About This Book

Why Is This Topic Important?

Influencing is something everyone needs to be able to do, but it requires a set of skills and understandings that is rarely taught explicitly. Since 1994, when we introduced our "influence fitness" program, Exercising Influence: Building Relationships and Getting Results, participants have asked for a book that they can read for further development. This book, as its name implies, is intended to be a practical guide to developing effective influencing skills independent of the seminar.

What Can You Achieve with This Book?

The book provides a means for reflecting on your current approach to influencing others, as well as examples, insights, tools, and skill practice opportunities that will help you to become a more effective influencer. You will develop a greater appreciation for the many opportunities you have daily to make your life and work more satisfying and meaningful through influential communication. You can use this book in several ways:

- As a general information book, to be read in its entirety.
- As a resource for specific ideas about various aspects of influencing. If you use it in this way, you may want to read the first part and then use the rest for reference, as appropriate.
- As a guide to a structured influence fitness program that can be implemented alone or with others in a conscious and sequential way for the purpose of developing and improving skills.
- As a follow-up to or preparation for attending the course, Exercising Influence: Building Relationships and Getting Results. For information on this course, see the first item in the Notes section.

How Is the Book Organized?

The material in this book is divided into three parts. The first part, Exercising Influence, focuses on developing the skills and understanding required to be an effective influencer. The second part, Planning for Influence, provides practical advice on preparing for, implementing, and reviewing an actual influence opportunity. The third part, Special Issues in Influence, explores important issues that arise in the process of exercising your influence, as well as special applications of influence skills. Each of the short chapters within the sections covers an area that is relevant to influencing in all aspects of life. The remainder of the book includes an Appendix with supplementary material.

There are two companion pieces to this book. The first is a self-study guide, which can be used independently or by working with a coaching partner. It follows this book, chapter by chapter, and will enable the reader to deepen his or her understanding of influence. Practice exercises are included for skill development. The second piece is a discussion guide for a series of facilitated conversations based on this book. If you are a formal or informal leader of a group or wish to form a group to discuss this topic, the guide will provide you with plans and support material to enhance the group's learning and your facilitation skills.

In this book, I have used several metaphors that offer parallels to this complex topic. Developing influence skills is like fitness training; the planning process is like preparing for a safari; and the actual experience of influencing is like improvisational theater. The process of becoming an effective influencer is a lifelong journey. To help guide us on this journey, I have selected some quotations from Ralph Waldo Emerson, whose wisdom and good sense speak to us across 170 years. Emerson's essays, most of them written in the 1830s and 1840s, are especially full of relevant observations and advice of value to those of us interested in building relationships and getting results through influence. In an 1844 essay, Emerson wrote, "This is that which we call character—a reserved force which acts directly by presence, and without means." That is as good a definition of the power of influence as we are likely to find.

About Pfeiffer

Pfeiffer serves the professional development and hands-on resource needs of training and human resource practitioners and gives them products to do their jobs better. We deliver proven ideas and solutions from experts in HR development and HR management, and we offer effective and customizable tools to improve workplace performance. From novice to seasoned professional, Pfeiffer is the source you can trust to make yourself and your organization more successful.

Essential Knowledge Pfeiffer produces insightful, practical, and comprehensive materials on topics that matter the most to training and HR professionals. Our Essential Knowledge resources translate the expertise of seasoned professionals into practical, how-to guidance on critical workplace issues and problems. These resources are supported by case studies, worksheets, and job aids and are frequently supplemented with CD-ROMs, websites, and other means of making the content easier to read, understand, and use.

Essential Tools Pfeiffer's Essential Tools resources save time and expense by offering proven, ready-to-use materials—including exercises, activities, games, instruments, and assessments—for use during a training or team-learning event. These resources are frequently offered in looseleaf or CD-ROM format to facilitate copying and customization of the material.

Pfeiffer also recognizes the remarkable power of new technologies in expanding the reach and effectiveness of training. While e-hype has often created whizbang solutions in search of a problem, we are dedicated to bringing convenience and enhancements to proven training solutions. All our e-tools comply with rigorous functionality standards. The most appropriate technology wrapped around essential content yields the perfect solution for today's on-the-go trainers and human resource professionals.

Pfeiffer
www.pfeiffer.com   *Essential resources for training and HR professionals*

This book is dedicated to Abigail, Elizabeth, Emily, and Isaac—the next generation of influencers.

Exercising Influence

Revised Edition

A Guide for Making Things Happen
at Work, at Home, and in Your Community

B. Kim Barnes

Pfeiffer
A Wiley Imprint
www.pfeiffer.com

Library of Congress Cataloging-in-Publication Data
Barnes, B. Kim.
  Exercising influence, revised edition: a guide for making things happen at work, at home, and in your community / B. Kim Barnes. — Rev.ed.
     p. cm.
  Includes bibliographical references and index.
  ISBN-13: 978-0-7879-8463-2 (pbk.)
  ISBN-10: 0-7879-8463-9 (pbk.)
  1. Influence (Psychology) 2. Persuasion (Psychology) 3. Compliance. I. Title.
  BF774.B265 2007
  153.8'5—dc22

                        2006014166

Acquiring Editor: Matthew Davis
Production Editor: Dawn Kilgore
Manufacturing Supervisor: Becky Carreño

Director of Development: Kathleen Dolan Davies
Editor: Rebecca Taff

Printing   10   9   8   7   6   5   4   3   2

Contents

Acknowledgments

I AM MOST GRATEFUL to those friends, colleagues, clients, and others who took the time to read and comment on the first edition of this book. I have been delighted to work with the Pfeiffer staff to develop this second edition.

My special thanks go to Cindy Coe and Guadalupe Guajardo, for their professional, yet kind-hearted reviews and excellent suggestions, and to Leslie Stephen for her helpful ideas and light touch as an editor.

Nobody could ask for a better team than the Barnes & Conti staff. I am particularly grateful to Roslyn Raley for her patience, precision, and amazing mind-reading skills in moving this project along.

Some of the material in this book is adapted with permission from Barnes & Conti's *Exercising Influence: Building Relationships and Getting Results*.[1] Developing and working with that program and with the extraordinary colleagues who facilitate it continues to be a wonderful learning experience. The many program participants who have shared their influence challenges and insights with all of us have contributed greatly to my personal development as an influencer and to this book.

It has been my very good fortune to work with two outstanding teachers and mentors in the field of interpersonal influence, David Berlew, Ph.D., and Roger Harrison, Ph.D. Without their knowledge and passion for the subject, this book would not have been written.

CHAPTER 1

What We've Got Here Is Failure to Influence . . .

"Shallow men believe in luck."

—Ralph Waldo Emerson

DO ANY OF THESE situations sound familiar to you?

- It's five o'clock. You have been at your desk since 6:00 this morning, and you're nowhere near ready to go home. You have a meeting with your manager tomorrow morning, and you're supposed to have a report finished. You would have, too, if the other people involved had done their parts. First, the data was late from your counterpart in the other group. The people on your team had other priorities and couldn't help you with the analysis. Then the "admin" was too busy to help you prepare a decent-looking presentation. You might have asked your manager for an extension, but you didn't want to look unprepared, so you decided to do it all yourself. It looks like an all-nighter.

- Your teenage daughter, a bright and successful student, has announced that she will be turning down a scholarship to a prestigious university in favor of taking a year off to travel and "find herself." You have had several heated arguments about this. Recently, you told her that you could not guarantee that you would pay her college tuition when she returned. Her response was that she was perfectly capable of earning her own money and attending a less expensive school. You feel that you have painted yourself into a corner and have not made any progress in convincing her of the importance to her future of making the right college choice. You are also concerned about her safety as a solo traveler in certain parts of the world.

- You are a senior executive who is charged with the responsibility for implementing the final steps in merging two companies. Executives of the other firm, who see this as an acquisition by your company rather than a merger, are dragging their feet in regard to getting their systems aligned with yours. They give you excuses that sound rational, but the net effect is to delay the implementation. You are under a lot of pressure to get this completed. The new, merged systems should have been up and running by now, and you are feeling very frustrated and angry.

- You have volunteered to help plan and host the yearly fundraiser for your child's preschool. You were reluctant to take this on for fear that you might end up, as has happened before, doing it all yourself. The first few meetings of your committee were very positive; several people volunteered to take responsibility for specific tasks. Now it is two weeks before the event, and several important things have not happened. Everyone has an excuse for not delivering on his or her commitments. You feel that the staff and board are depending on you, and you don't want to let them down. This experience has convinced you, however, that you are not cut out for community leadership. You feel burned out and disappointed.

- You have been nurturing an idea for a couple of years now. It would be an application of your current technology that you believe would have a tremendous impact on the market. It would require a moderate commitment of resources, but the payoff could be spectacular. The problem is that such a project is outside of your current area of responsibility and, in fact, might be seen as competitive with another group's current project. Your manager has already told you that you would have to have it approved and funded elsewhere; you suspect it is a political "hot potato." You are still hoping that someone will recognize the potential and support it, but you are discouraged.

- You were recently offered an exciting new position with your company. It would involve spending three years abroad and would probably lead to a significant role for you in the company's future. When you told your spouse about it, you expected enthusiastic support. Instead, you received a flat and resistant response. This surprised you, as you have always agreed that whichever one of you was offered the best opportunity would have the other's support, regardless of any inconvenience and disruption that might occur.

- You are the leader for an important project for your company. The project is not going as well as you had hoped. There is a lot of conflict, and milestones are not being achieved. You were selected for this role because of your technical skills, but what is dragging you down is the day-to-day hassle of dealing with people's egos and working out the turf issues that seem to get in the way of every cross-functional team you have worked with.

- You are chairing a standards task force for your association that could make a major impact on the conduct of your profession. Some members of the group are very resistant to the idea of mandatory compliance with the standards. You and several others believe that it is an exercise in futility to develop and present standards and then let people choose whether to adopt them or not. The differences have divided the group, which has now reached an impasse. If you do not come to an agreement, the entire exercise will be seen as a waste of time. You feel that you will lose the respect of your colleagues, both within the task force and outside of it; they have been counting on you to resolve this issue.

The Value of Influence Skills

If you have experienced anything like any of the situations above, you know that all of your competence and skill will not resolve many of the human issues involved in getting technical, business, or personal results that are important to you and others. In the real world, a good idea doesn't necessarily sell itself. People don't always share the same values, priorities, and vested interests, even though they work for the same company, share a profession, or live in the same community or household. If you want to be successful as a leader, manager, colleague, friend, spouse, parent, or partner, you must be able to achieve results through the effort and support of others. This requires a good set of influence skills. You already know a lot about influence—we all use it and are affected by the way others use it. By reading this book, practicing, and reflecting, you will bring the process of influence to your conscious attention and learn to manage it with greater focus, precision, ease, and effectiveness.

As a business or technical leader, you are charged with the responsibility for getting results through others—frequently those over whom you do not exercise direct control. Although this is a common expectation, you may not have received any training or preparation for the tough issues and challenges that come with this territory.

As a member of a team, family, club, or other small group, you know that they seldom operate on the basis of hierarchical power or seniority (though you might sometimes wish they would, especially if you are a parent, a committee chair, or a team leader). You may not have many role models for influencing effectively in this kind of environment.

Skillful influencing is more than just effective communication. It is possible to communicate often and clearly without achieving your desired results. These skills can be learned, but success as an influencer also requires you to have the ability to read the person and the situation—and the discipline to hold a clear goal in mind while selecting and using the behaviors that are likely to lead you toward that goal. There are many opportunities in daily life to exercise your influence.

A good set of influence skills can lead to:

- Improved ability to manage and lead cross-functionally

- More positive and productive personal and professional relationships

- Greater ability to choose and use behaviors tactically to achieve strategic objectives

- More confidence in your ability to achieve results through other people and a better track record of actually doing so

- Increased flexibility in dealing with people from diverse professional and cultural backgrounds, as well as those who differ from you in gender, generation, experience, and personality

- Improved skills for resolving conflict

In this book, we will explore some practical ideas and tools for exercising influence in all aspects of your life. Influence involves sophisticated understandings and a complex set of skills. Some situations are fairly straightforward and require little in the way of planning; others are Byzantine in their complexity. We don't always get to choose which influence opportunities we will be confronted with. I have tried to cover, at least briefly, the major areas that are useful for the influencer to explore. Not all of them will be relevant to or needed for every influence situation. I hope you will find enough here to stimulate your interest in influence and increase your confidence as an influencer. The best way to learn it, of course, is to do it.

CHAPTER 2

What Is Influence, and Why Do We Want to Have It?

"All that Adam had, all that Caesar could, you have and can do. . . . Build, therefore, your own world."

—Ralph Waldo Emerson

Influence and Power

The word "power" is a noun that indicates ability, strength, and authority. "Influence" is most often used as a verb, meaning to sway or induce another to take action. (It can also be used as a noun, often interchangeably with power.) In this book, we will consider power to be something you *have* and influence to be something you *do*. Electric power exists only as a potential source of light in your home or office until you flip a switch (or activate a beam that does the switching). Likewise, your power exists only as potential until you activate the sources through the use of influence.

Many sources of power are available to you. Among them are

- Formal authority associated with your role, job, or office

- Referred or delegated power from a person or a group that you represent

- Information, skill, or expertise

- Reputation for achievements and ability to get things done

- Relationships and mutual obligations

- Moral authority, based on the respect and admiration of others for the way that you act on your principles

- Personal power, based on self-confidence and commitment to an idea

Power may be used directly (for example, "You are going to bed now because I am your mother and I say so") or indirectly, through others (for example, "Let Jack know in a subtle way that I would prefer the other vendor"). If the demanding party's power is understood, and considered legitimate and sufficient from the point of view of the responding party, the action will happen. In general, when power is called for, it is better to use it directly to avoid confusion, delay, or doubt. Power used indirectly can sometimes be experienced as manipulation. Many situations call for the direct use of power. Emergencies and other situations in which rapid decision making is essential are times when fast and effective action is more important than involvement and commitment.

In day-to-day life, the direct use of power has several limitations.

- Others must perceive your power as legitimate, sufficient, and appropriate to the situation.

- The use of power seldom changes minds or hearts; thus you cannot count on follow-up that you are not there to supervise.

- The direct use of power does not invite others to take a share of the responsibility for the outcome. Others do not have the opportunity to grow by having to make decisions and live with the consequences.

Influence behavior uses your sources of power to move another person toward making a choice or commitment that supports a goal you wish to achieve. Various sources of power will be appropriate with different people and in different situations. They will support the use of a variety of influence skills. Using influence rather than direct power sends a message of respect to the other. It results in action by the other that is voluntary rather than coerced; quality and timelines are likely to be better. It is also the realistic choice to make in the many situations we encounter in which we need to get things done through other people over whom we have no legitimate power.

Influence and Leadership

Leaders must be able to use both approaches—direct power and influence skills—and must know when each is appropriate. Few leaders are satisfied with blind obedience (obedience in adults is never "blind"—it is an emergency response, a fear response, or betrays a lack of interest in and responsibility for the outcome). Most leaders want to work with people who are willing to influence as well as to be influenced.

Because influence tends to be reciprocal, part of a relationship, it is important for a leader to let others know when and how he or she can be influenced on an issue. A big mistake often made by leaders and managers is to act as if they can be influenced (for example, by asking people what they think about something) and then communicating (often by arguing with their suggestions) that the decision has already been made. Presumably, the leader was hoping that people would come to the same—obvious to the leader—conclusion, so that they would be committed to the decision. This only creates cynicism and has given "participatory management" and "employee empowerment" bad names. If you have to use direct power, use it with confidence, not apologetically. Then involve people about something related to the issue, where you can be influenced. For example, suppose that a reorganization will occur whether your direct reports want it to happen or not. Although you might be tempted to try to develop support for the action by seeming to engage others in the decision, you know that would be inappropriate given the fact that the decision has already been made. Announce it and give people time to absorb the news, express concerns, and ask questions. Then ask, "What support will you need from me to communicate about this and plan transitions for your employees?"

Successful leaders learn and practice a wide variety of influence behaviors. They keep the goal in front of them and act in a way that is consistent with the aim of achieving that result, through and with others. Leadership in a team, family, or community organization is usually shared. The option to use direct power is often less available or effective, yet the responsibilities remain. Those in both formal and informal leadership roles must call on their personal influence skills to align other members toward a shared goal and to energize and inspire them to do what it takes to achieve it.

Your Sphere of Influence

Each of us has a "sphere of influence." This includes issues and areas over which we exercise control, those where we can directly influence the outcome, and those where we can influence the situation indirectly through other people or as part of a group.

Use Figure 2.1 to chart your current sphere of influence. In which aspects of your life can you control an outcome by yourself?

Figure 2.1.   Sphere of Influence

What issues in your life are open to influence that you can exercise directly? Where do you have the opportunity to influence a situation indirectly by getting another person or a group to do the direct influence? What are the areas and issues in your life that are important to you, but where you see no opportunity to influence?

As you review your chart, notice how active a role you are taking in influencing the outcome of issues and events that you care about. Is there anything about which you care deeply that you perceive as being outside of your sphere of influence entirely? Many people find that their areas of direct control are limited to choices about their own behavior, but that it is possible to influence, either directly or indirectly, many events and outcomes in which they hold a strong interest.

Typical examples for sphere of control might include:

- What to wear (what is "business casual," anyway?)
- The order in which you do certain things
- The level of your own commitment
- Your own behavioral choices, for example, how to communicate with or influence someone
- How to organize your workspace or closet

These are choices you can make on your own—no one else needs to be involved or consulted (although you may opt to involve or consult others).

Your sphere of direct influence may include issues involving:

- Family members
- Friends
- Manager
- Team members
- Peers
- Direct reports

- Internal and external customers

- Neighbors

- Vendors

- Neighborhood business owners

- Local government officials

- Local media

- Members and leaders of professional and community organizations of which you are a member

In these cases, you can go directly to the person or group you wish to influence and use your skills to achieve the results that are of interest to you.

Your sphere of indirect influence may include:

- Senior managers in your company

- Other department heads

- Regional and national government officials who represent you in some way

- Competitors

- The leadership of large companies with which you do business

- Your customers' customers

- The national media

You may be able to have an impact on them through others who are in a position to influence them directly; through organizing a group to influence together; or through the act of voting, organizing an e-mail or letter-writing campaign, or other means.

Most of us would acknowledge that we have little or no influence in areas such as the global economy, a competitor's business strategy, large-scale trends such as industry consolidation, or decisions made by leaders of countries we don't live in, any more than we do the weather. Yet these and other decisions and events can have an impact on our lives and on how we influence. For example, knowing that a certain industry is having difficulty filling orders because of shortages of a raw material from a country that is at war may affect our approach to negotiating a business deal. We may not have any impact on the route a hurricane will take, but we can use information we have heard about it to influence a relative's travel plans.

Empowerment: Buzzword or Reality?

If asked, most people would say they do not want control over other people—but neither do they want others to have control over them. Research on work-related stress has demonstrated that those with low power and high responsibility have the greatest levels of stress.[2] Our physiological "fight or flight" response is intensified when we feel the pressure to take action but do not have the legitimacy or the resources to make something happen. Organizations in which people feel they have little influence over matters that affect them become "cultures of complaint." For example, I remember two trips I made to the former Soviet Union, about two years apart. During the first trip, just before the ascent of Gorbachev and the liberalization of the totalitarian government, I was struck by the fact that few people tried to talk to us. When they did, they asked questions about life in the United States, but rarely shared information about their own lives. Two years later, it was easy to see that glasnost, or openness, was working; people talked with us constantly about their lives. However, perestroika (restructuring) clearly was not yet a reality. Thus, nearly all the conversations consisted of stories about how bad things were or what terrible things the government had done to them or to their parents. They now knew and could talk about everything—but did not feel that they could do anything about it—so they complained.

While there has been much discussion in organizations and families about empowerment, the reality is that, as individuals and groups, we cannot wait passively for others to give us power. Organizations, institutions, and leaders may offer us power, but we can use it only when we have created and accepted empowerment for ourselves. Accepting empowerment means accepting responsibility for the outcome of our actions. As a buzzword, empowerment has probably run its course—but as a concept, it has a lot of life left. In most organizations and families these days, true empowerment means an openness to influence from and in all directions.

In today's information-based organizations, direct power and control are rare commodities. Particularly in competitive, global organizations, decisions must be made on the basis of complex information drawn from a variety of sources. Governance of the organization is often broad-based. Much of the work of these organizations occurs across functions, outside of formal hierarchies, sometimes by teams of people who rarely, if ever, meet face-to-face. Increasingly, people who are empowered to take action make decisions across boundaries of space, time, and nationality.

Families today are less hierarchical. In North America, Australia, New Zealand, and much of Western and Central Europe, the typical family is a complex unit made up of individuals with a variety of sources of power and levels of responsibility. Typically, family roles are more fluid than in the past. In many families, both parents work; in some of those cases each person may have a career that is very important to him or her. In single-parent families, where the parent is working, children may assume greater responsibilities. Traditional extended families are often less available or geographically convenient, especially in North America. Children may have information and economic power bases that enable them to participate in family decisions on a more equal basis than in the past, when parents and grandparents were keepers of traditions, knowledge, and authority. (Any family that owns a computer knows that the power balance in families has changed.) Peer groups offer an alternative source of need satisfaction for children and adolescents, rendering the nuclear family less powerful, whether we like it or not.

In communities, also, the traditional power relationships in Western society have broken down. There is no overarching institution, like the church in medieval society or Tammany Hall in turn-of-the-20th-Century New York, to provide the final word on what can and should be done. Instead, there are multiple competing interest groups, each with its own set of problems and preferred solutions. It sometimes seems that the community is divided into tiny fractions, each with a particular vested interest around which to organize. Yet, people from many cultural, religious, occupational, economic, and educational backgrounds must be able to come to agreement on solutions to problems that affect all of them.

In today's more open and empowered organizations and societies, opportunities for exerting influence and power abound for those who are willing to accept the attendant responsibilities and accountabilities.

Benefits and Costs of Exercising Influence

In this complex, multi-ethnic society, individuals must depend on their interpersonal skills to build coalitions and make things happen with and through the other people within their spheres of influence. The benefits are clear—you can achieve goals that you could not accomplish by yourself and reduce the stress associated with having a lot of responsibility without sufficient resources to do the job. You can create visibility and opportunity for yourself and for ideas, causes, or projects that are important to you.

For example, you may be responsible at work or in your community for a project that does not have its own budget. In order to achieve the results you hope and are expected to accomplish, you will have to beg, borrow, or steal the resources that are required. You will need to influence the right people to take an interest in your project's success and be willing to contribute time, energy, equipment, people, or money to make it happen.

Or perhaps you would like to purchase a vacation home, but you know that it will require some voluntary sacrifices on the part of everyone in the family to make it a reality. You may have to forego regular vacations for a couple of years. You will have to influence the rest of the family to share your vision and trade off near-term pleasures for longer-term satisfaction.

I remember a client who called me in despair one day to report that he was near exhaustion; nobody seemed willing to help him complete a long report that was due the following week, and he did not know how he was going to finish in time. I asked him what he had done to get some support from his teammates. He answered, "They can see that I am over my head and nobody has offered to do a thing." "Yes," I said, "but have you asked them?" He allowed that he had not. The next day, he called back to report that everyone he had asked had been willing to do something. "They thought I didn't need help," he said, wonderingly.

The story above illustrates an obvious benefit. Making the effort to influence can pay off in many ways. At the same time, exercising influence can be costly in time and effort, and sometimes in other, more subtle ways. Once we have become active in influencing a particular outcome, we may create expectations on the part of others that we will continue to champion certain ideas and values. By taking an active role, we may also face more in the way of conflict and feel that we have to accept greater responsibility. It is always useful to balance the costs and benefits when deciding whether it is worth putting forth the energy required to influence.

Where Should We Exercise Influence?

Although some issues at work, at home, and in community activities are appropriately handled through the use of direct power or simple communication, many others lend themselves particularly well to influence. Influence issues are ones that require mutual agreement and commitment.

Typical workplace influence issues include:

- Getting support for ideas

- Assigning responsibilities in a team

- Acquiring needed resources for a project

- Being assigned to interesting projects or career development opportunities

Some family or household issues that lend themselves well to influence include:

- Distributing chores, tasks, and responsibilities

- Planning for vacations or outings

- Assigning proportions of costs for shared activities or household expenses

- Making decisions about major purchases

In community activities, almost everything is subject to influence, since most people are volunteering their time. Examples include:

- Convincing the right people to serve on a committee

- Gaining agreement on principles and processes

- Getting people to deliver on commitments

- Managing disagreements and conflicts

Developing and Improving Influence Fitness

All of us learn early in our lives how to influence the people who are most important to our well-being. As infants, we have only a few means of communicating our needs and wants. Gradually, we develop a complete set of influence muscles. Toddlers experiment with a wide variety of means to exert influence. Through observation, education, experience, and experimentation, we tend to develop a favored set of influence skills—ones that we have been most exposed to or that have worked the best for us. As long as we remain within the context (family, culture, school, workplace) where we have been successful as influencers, there is little need to develop some of the underused or rejected skills. However, when we embark on new experiences, encounter new problems, or meet new people, we may find that our present levels of expertise do not allow us the flexibility we need to be successful.

In our workshops, we view developing influence skills as analogous to developing physical fitness. You have all the muscles you will ever need, but a good fitness program helps you build and develop them

so you can be more powerful, graceful, and flexible—in greater
control of your own physical and mental well-being. Similarly, you
already have all the basic influence muscles you need, but some of
them are probably underdeveloped or flabby due to lack of use. A
purposeful program for developing influence fitness can also enable
you to become more powerful, graceful, and flexible—more effective
as a person at work, at home, and in your community.

Reading this book can introduce you to the concepts involved
in conscious and effective influencing, especially if you do so with
specific influence opportunities in mind. But only by practicing the
behaviors in a safe environment, where you can count on receiving
honest feedback, will you truly develop those influence muscles.
(See Appendix A for some suggestions about setting up a coaching
partnership.)

CHAPTER 3

A Model for Exercising Influence:

Building Relationships and Getting Results

"The life of a [person] is a self-evolving circle, which, from a ring imperceptibly small, rushes on all sides outward to new and larger circles, and that without end. . . . The extent to which this generation of circles . . . will go depends on the force or truth of the individual soul."
—Ralph Waldo Emerson

A Framework for Influence

Influencing others successfully is a complex process. It is not enough to be interpersonally skillful. There is nothing you can do or say that will guarantee success every time with every person in every situation. However, you can help yourself to succeed in challenging influence situations like the ones described at the beginning of this book by considering the entire framework of your influence opportunity. Figure 3.1 represents an effective framework for thinking about influence. There are four elements within the framework. These are

1. *Results:* What are you hoping to accomplish through influencing this person?

2. *Relationship:* What kind of influence relationship do you currently have?

Figure 3.1. **Influence Framework**

Exercising Influence, Revised Edition. Copyright © 2007 by John Wiley & Sons, Inc. Reproduced by permission of Pfeiffer, an Imprint of Wiley. www.pfeiffer.com

3. *Context:* What individual, organizational, or cultural issues might affect the results?

4. *Approach:* Which influence tactics and behaviors are the most likely to help you accomplish your goal?

Of course, influence does not take place within a closed system. External elements such as trends and issues in the environment may also have an impact on the outcome. These elements, over which you have no control, may, however, lead you to change or adapt your approach or timing.

This chapter will give you an overview of each of the elements in the influence framework. In Part II, each of these elements will be developed more fully, with suggestions as to how you can apply the information to a real influence opportunity.

Results: What Would Success Look Like?

When thinking about an influence opportunity, the best place to start is where you would like to end up. What result do you hope to achieve by influencing this person or group? How will you know that you have been successful? What will you see, hear, or experience that will let you know you have accomplished your goal?

Sometimes we are embarrassed or ashamed to acknowledge, even to ourselves, that we want results—pretty specific results at that— and will be deeply disappointed if we don't obtain them. When we don't approve of our own wish to influence, we might be manipulative or half-hearted about the process, hoping to get away with it without anyone—even ourselves—noticing. And, of course, that doesn't work very well. So if you care about the outcome of a discussion, a meeting, a proposal, a request, or a family council, let yourself know it. When you can do this, you have started along the path of conscious influencing. You won't always be successful, but you will probably find that you feel stronger, less stressed, and more powerful, because you are taking an active role, rather than playing the victim of circumstances or of other people's actions or decisions.

Influence goals are based on needs and requirements that can often be met in a variety of ways. There will be times when you will change your specific influence goal in order to be more certain of achieving a result that will meet your needs. In Chapter 8, you will learn how to design an influence goal that will be a good "star to steer by."

Relationships: How Well Do You Influence One Another?

A key element in your influence framework is the relationship you have developed with the person you wish to influence. An influence relationship exists, potentially, when one or both parties have goals that require the support or actions of the other. Not all relationships are influence relationships. There are people with whom we communicate regularly, but whose actions are irrelevant to our own goals. It is possible to have a good friendship with someone without having an effective influence relationship with that person, and it is possible to have a good influence relationship with someone you would not choose as a friend. Since influencing another person is not an event, but part of a process, everything that occurs in your influence relationship affects the future of that relationship. The success or failure of subsequent influence opportunities with that person depends on the influence history you build together. If the other person or group feels that you were not fair or honest in your dealings, you will become less influential.

When you can assess the state of the relationship honestly and accurately, you will know whether or not the other person is likely to be open to being influenced by you. If that is unlikely, you will have to begin by doing the work that is required to repair or rebuild your influence relationship—or decide to influence indirectly through another person or group.

An influence relationship at work or in the community is not necessarily a close personal friendship. You may have few social interests in common or have the wrong chemistry to be friends. The basic criterion for choosing someone with whom to build an influence relationship is that there is some mutual benefit possible if you are willing and able to help or support one another.

In this complex and changing world, building solid and mutually beneficial influence relationships within your organization and profession, as well as outside of it, creates a network of information and opportunity that you will be able to call on throughout your professional life. Building positive influence relationships in your family and community will provide you with a lifelong base of support. Paradoxically, the very time that you need a good influence relationship the most is likely to be the hardest time to start building one. Successful influencers are aware of this; not only do they avoid burning bridges they may need to cross one day, but they put effort into building bridges before they are needed.

Chapter 9 will help you to better understand and to build and improve on your existing influence relationships. You will also gain some ideas on developing new and effective influence relationships.

Context: What Else Is Going On?

Influence does not occur in a vacuum. There are always many factors in the situation that can affect the outcome. In general, these factors can be found in three areas.

1. Individual (both yourself and the person you want to influence)

   - *Personality and preferences:* Where is the "comfort zone" for each of us? How does he or she prefer to be influenced? What is my usual approach?

- *Values and goals:* What is important to each of us? What is riding on this influence opportunity?

- *Current issues and priorities:* Where is the other's attention focused right now? Is this a good time to influence?

- *Needs and vested interests:* What does each of us have to gain or lose by the outcome?

2. Organizational

- *Purpose and vision:* What is the organization about? How can I align my influence issue with the business goals?

- *Structure and processes:* How does the organization work? What do I need to know in order to get a hearing?

- *Power relationships:* What are the current politics of the organization? Who is important to the success of my influence opportunity?

- *Current issues and priorities:* What is important right now? How can I use that to increase the relevance of my approach?

3. Cultural (national, professional, community, or organizational)

- *Values:* What does the organization or group believe to be right, good, or important? What is the basis for decisions?

- *Norms:* What is the "right way" to get things done?

- *Taboos:* What is outside the boundaries of the acceptable?

You will want to spend some time thinking about how your own needs and vested interests, personality, and behavioral skills affect the context for influence with this particular person, organization, and/or culture. Chapters 10, 11, and 12 treat these issues in more depth and provide ideas and practical suggestions for dealing with each aspect of the context for influence.

Approach: How Will I Achieve Results?

Once you have established a realistic but optimistic goal, considered the state of the relationship, and analyzed the contextual factors, you are in a good position to select the tactical approach and specific behaviors that are most likely to accomplish the results you hope to achieve.

Direct influence behaviors fall into two categories: *expressive* influence and *receptive* influence. Expressive influence behaviors involve sending ideas and information toward others in a way that will engage their interest and persuade them to support you. Receptive influence behaviors involve drawing ideas and information from others in a way that will guide them toward a commitment to action. The influence model in Figure 3.2 shows the expressive and receptive influence tactics.

Neither type of influence behavior is better or worse than the other one. Each of the behaviors is intended to accomplish a particular influence result. Used thoughtfully, in combination, they can lead you toward achieving your influence goals. Over time, often within the same conversation, you will aim to balance expressive and receptive influence energy. (In Chapter 14, you will learn some guidelines for selecting and using specific behaviors.)

Figure 3.2.   Influence Model

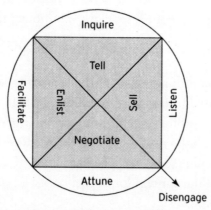

Table 3.1 shows the influence tactics and behaviors and what they are designed to accomplish. You'll notice two columns: tactics and behaviors. The *intention* is what you want your behavior to achieve. The *tactic* is a summary of the intention. The *behaviors* are specific ways of implementing the tactics.

Table 3.1.   Influence Tactics and Behavior

Expressive

Tactics	Behaviors
Tell: Communicate the desired action	Suggest Express needs
Sell: Convince the other to commit to action	Offer reasons Refer to shared values or goals
Negotiate: Give the other a vested interest in taking action	Offer incentives Describe consequences
Enlist: Create enthusiasm and alignment	Envision Encourage

Receptive

Tactics	Behaviors
Inquire: Get information or involvement; guide the other's thinking	Ask open-ended questions Draw out
Listen: Learn real limits or expand the other's thinking	Check understanding Test implications
Attune: Build trust or increase openness	Identify with other Disclose
Facilitate: Get the other to take responsibility for action	Clarify issues Pose challenging questions
Disengage	Live to influence another day

Influence behaviors have both verbal and nonverbal components. Facial expression, voice tone, gestures, and the way you use space can all contribute to or detract from the impact of your influence.

Using any influence behavior effectively requires, first of all, being clear about the results you want to obtain—your influence goal. Next, you will think about the person you are going to influence and the influence relationship you currently have with one another. You will consider the context in which the influence will take place: individual, team, organizational, or cultural factors and issues that might affect the outcome. You can select the tactics and then the behaviors that are most likely to be useful under the circumstances and even plan a specific approach. However, during the actual influence event, you will stay alert to the other's responses and monitor whether you are moving closer to or further from your goal— or approaching an alternate result that meets your needs satisfactorily.

In Chapters 4 and 5, you will explore the specific influence behaviors in greater depth. In Chapter 14, you will learn how to choose and use influence behaviors to achieve specific results.

What Is the Issue?

Some influence opportunities are focused on personal preferences and priorities. Some, however, involve deep and complex issues that require study and exploration. Influence opportunities that are related to a specific problem that is owned or shared by the other person may require you to develop a thorough understanding of the issues involved. Chapter 13 provides some suggestions as to how to prepare for influence situations that involve complex issues.

CHAPTER 4

Expressive Influence

Sending Ideas and Generating Energy

"Nothing great was ever accomplished without enthusiasm."
—Ralph Waldo Emerson

The Purpose of Expressive Influence

Expressive influence sends your ideas and energy out to others. Many people think of influence as primarily an expressive activity— one in which they are continually sending ideas and information toward others. In fact, effective influence requires a balance of expressive and receptive activity, as does any form of communication.

Too many people overuse or misuse expressive influence. You have probably been in meetings where long-windedness, repetitive- ness, and an excruciating level of detail caused you to leave the room mentally or physically without absorbing or being influenced by a single idea. In these "meetings from hell," there was probably little or no opportunity to ask a question or make a comment that might have sparked a productive discussion. Often, the speaker involved in such a meeting is unaware of his or her impact (or lack of it) because he or she is focused internally on what to say next, rather than attend- ing to whether or not the current words are having an impact.

On the other hand, you may have had the good fortune to listen to someone who stimulated your thinking with an exciting idea, changed your mind through an excellent argument, made you an offer you didn't want to refuse, or inspired you to believe that you could accomplish great things.

Expressive influence, used effectively, can lead people to action. It is especially effective when people are uncertain about what to do and have respect for and trust in the person who is influencing. The use of expressive influence can communicate to others that you mean business and are to be taken seriously. It allows you to communicate your enthusiasm for an idea or belief and exhort others to share it.

The Expressive Behaviors

Figure 4.1 shows the specific tactics and behaviors associated with expressive influence. The expressive tactics in this model are named according to what they are intended to do. They include tell, sell, negotiate, and enlist.

Figure 4.1.   Expressive Influence Tactics and Behaviors

1. You can *tell* by making a suggestion or by expressing your needs.

   - "Let's meet twice a month on the standards issue until we are ready to present the report." (Suggest)

   - "I need your input on the plans by Friday." (Express needs)

2. You can *sell* by offering reasons or by referring to shared values and goals.

   - "That way, we can meet the deadline for the report." (Offer reasons)

   - "With both of us contributing, we should be able to achieve our goal of completing the plan before the end of the quarter." (Refer to shared values or goals)

3. You can *negotiate* by offering incentives or by describing consequences.

   - "If you will extend the deadline by a week, I will provide you with an outline of the major conclusions that you can use for your meeting." (Offer incentives)

   - "I need to let you know that if you are not ready by 7 o'clock tomorrow, I will not be able to drive you to school." (Describe consequences)

4. You can *enlist* by envisioning a desired future or by encouraging the other person to join you.

   - "I can see this team creating the product that finally puts this company on the map." (Envision)

   - "You are exactly the person who can attract the best candidate. You have a special ability to communicate the exciting work we want to do here." (Encourage)

How Expressive Behaviors Work

- *Tell* behaviors influence by letting others know what you want and need from them. Often, people will be willing to help and support your efforts if they know what you would like them to do.

- *Sell* behaviors influence by showing people reasons for and benefits from them taking an action.

- *Negotiate* behaviors influence by offering others a fair exchange for taking or refraining from taking an action.

- *Enlist* behaviors influence by creating enthusiasm and putting the other "in the picture."

Nonverbal Components of Expressive Behaviors

Expressive gestures, at least in Western cultures, are confident, free, and direct (although pointing your finger at someone while speaking will be perceived as aggressive and should be avoided). Try not to tilt your head; it is a basic mammalian signal indicating, "I acknowledge your superiority." (Watch the neighborhood dogs as they work out the hierarchy. We do the same thing, only we are a little subtler about it.) Smiling while using tell, sell, or negotiate behaviors can indicate uncertainty and nervousness. (Smiling is a natural and appropriate expression of enthusiasm while enlisting.) Eye contact should be used carefully with expressive influence. Too much of it may be perceived as challenging and aggressive. Direct eye contact is best used at key points, when you want to add emphasis. The rest of the time, you can look at the other person's forehead or cheekbones. This is polite, but not invasive.

Your posture should be relaxed but erect and balanced. My aikido[3] teacher once pointed out that the Japanese concept of "hara" or center was located in a space about 2 inches below your navel. He said that you should feel your weight centered there. If you are centered in your chest, you will seem aggressive; if in your head, placating. Keep both feet on the floor. (I know your fourth-grade teacher told you this. Do it anyway; it makes you look much more confident. Try it.) Standing up can add to your effectiveness, especially if you are physically smaller than the person or group you are influencing. Using a flip chart or whiteboard can make this a natural part of the discussion.

Your voice should come from as low as possible in your register; breathing helps. The emotional (and vocal) tone that works with expressive influence is businesslike and matter-of-fact, unless you are enlisting. Then you will use more colorful language and variable inflection. A sarcastic, negative, or hostile tone is likely to create a defensive reaction in the other person, who will conclude that you are not interested in two-way influence. Ending a sentence with an upward inflection may indicate uncertainty or a lack of confidence in what you are expressing, at least in some societies. (This may account for some misunderstandings between Canadians, who often use that inflection conversationally, and other English speakers.)

Using Expressive Influence at Work

Expressive influence is particularly useful at work early in a project or process, whether as part of a one-to-one conversation or in a meeting. The most obvious use of expressive behavior at work is simply to let others know what you want or need them to do. A good deal of time could be saved in most organizations if we were clearer with one another about this. Unfortunately, we are often reluctant to ask directly for what we want—sometimes because we are not sure it is legitimate to ask for it, sometimes because we are afraid of a direct "no," sometimes because we don't want the implicit or explicit responsibilities that would accompany an open agreement.

Meetings can be dull and unproductive when participants are unwilling to express opinions and ideas. This may be because of hidden conflict or fear of upsetting the status quo. People are also sometimes afraid to express ideas because of political or cultural concerns about whether they have the right to speak up and whether others will listen. Meetings that are consciously designed to stimulate a balance of expressive and receptive behaviors are most likely to be productive. (See Appendix C for suggested meeting process designs.)

Many conflicts in organizations arise because we are not explicit in expressing our needs and then become upset when we don't get what we want. We go away from meetings with an idea of who will do what by when, but then find that others interpreted the agreement differently. We do several favors for a colleague, believing that he or she "owes us one," but when we try to collect a return favor, we find that the other person has been keeping a different set of accounts. We believe strongly in a course of action and are deeply disappointed when we can't convince or inspire others to join us.

All of these issues might have been prevented by the thoughtful use of expressive influence behavior:

- "I'd like you to meet with me every week to review progress." (Express needs)

- "If you will take responsibility for finding a meeting space, I will gather and publish the agenda." (Offer incentives)

- "I would be glad to spend a day training your assistant on that. In exchange, I'd like you to assign her to our team for a day next week to help us complete our project report." (Offer incentives)

- "Here's what I see as possible. Six months from now we are all able to find every piece of data we need within minutes because we have agreed on a single database system that will work for all of us." (Envision)

Using Expressive Influence at Home

At home, the use of expressive influence is often complicated by the thought, "I shouldn't have to tell him or her that." We sometimes act as though mind-reading is a test of familial devotion. Psychologists have introduced us to the concept of the "double bind." ("I don't want you to clean up your room. I want you to WANT to clean up your room." In a double-bind situation, whichever choice you make is going to be the wrong one. If the child cleans up at the parent's request, that will not meet the parent's need—nor, of course, will ignoring the request.)

Using conscious and effective influence behavior at home is a good antidote to the complexities of family or household communication. A good influence goal (see Chapter 8) has to be observable in the short term, so you know whether you are on the right track or whether it would be better to take another approach. You can hear whether or not your housemate, son, or daughter has committed to clean the room. And you can see quite shortly afterward whether the room is clean (if you don't look in the closets or under the bed). And you will probably learn to be pretty satisfied with that, because it cuts down on a lot of unproductive conflict and aggravation.

- "I'd like you to help me with the yard work this morning." (Express needs)

- "There are two reasons why I suggested that we stick to long weekends rather than taking a longer vacation this summer. First, that will allow us to save enough to buy a boat for next summer, and secondly, that will mean I will have enough vacation days left for us to take a skiing vacation this winter." (Offer reasons or refer to shared values and goals; the impact would depend on whether the other person is interested in boats or skiing)

- "If you will agree to get a job that will pay for your room and board, I'll take responsibility for tuition and books." (Offer incentives)

- "It's a tough situation, but I see you as the kind of person who can inspire your peers to do the right thing. I remember how you got them to support the volunteer program." (Encourage)

Using Expressive Influence in Your Community

In our work in community organizations, we are often sensitive to the fact that people are not being paid to do the work that we want them to do or to take the stand that we wish they would. We may err on the side of vagueness rather than sound as if we are trying to be "the boss." Knowing that the only rewards for work in community service or religious organizations or political action groups are intangible satisfactions and others' appreciation, we tend to "go easy," rather than risk the loss of support and help. This can lead to a lack of energy and direction in the group or organization.

- "I believe in this project, and I'm willing to take responsibility for getting us started. Now I need two people who will work with me, starting today." (Express needs)

- "We are all committed to selecting the most qualified person for this important role. I believe Maria's credentials will stand up against that criterion." (Refer to shared values or goals)

- "If you are not willing to agree to put our name out there in support of this initiative, I will lose respect for this organization—and I believe that others will, too." (Describe consequences)

- "Here's what I anticipate. We are going to emerge from this crisis as a strong, united team, ready to lead this organization in an exciting new direction." (Envision)

When to Use Expressive Behaviors

As stated earlier, expressive and receptive behaviors work together, not in isolation from one another. Overall, you will strive for a balance of the two. Each kind of behavior has value and accomplishes certain specific results.

In summary, use expressive influence behaviors at work, at home, and in your community when:

- You want people to know what you need

- You have a solution to a problem that has been expressed by the other

- The conversation does not seem to be going anywhere

- You want to generate enthusiasm and energy

- You want to bring disagreements out in the open

- You want to move toward completing an agreement or gaining a commitment

Learning to be clear, direct, and straightforward in your expressive influence takes courage and confidence. It is easiest when you have done your homework, considering both facts and legitimate needs. It's also important that you be as prepared to listen respectfully to others' opinions and ideas as you hope they are to listen to yours. In the next chapter, you will learn about the behaviors that will help you to do this.

CHAPTER 5

Receptive Influence

Inviting Ideas and Stimulating Action

"Explore and explore. Be neither chided nor flattered out of your position of perpetual inquiry. Neither dogmatize [nor] accept another's dogmatism."

—Ralph Waldo Emerson

The Purpose of Receptive Influence

Receptive influence invites others to contribute ideas, information, and action. Since most people tend to overuse expressive behaviors when they wish to influence, they also tend to under-use receptive behaviors—behaviors that they may use very effectively and un-self-consciously as part of everyday conversations with friends and family, coaching or counseling sessions, or intellectual discussions. It is not obvious to everyone that receptive behaviors offer an effective way to influence others directly.

Receptive behaviors, used skillfully, can guide you and others toward an agreement, solution, or choice that satisfies each of you. You cannot really influence a person to do something that he or she knows to be against his or her best interests, since influence implies choice, unless you are appealing to a negative and vulnerable aspect of that person. (This is discussed in Chapter 16 on the ethics of influence).

Receptive influence indicates respect for the ideas and concerns of the other person and acknowledges his or her authority and accountabilities. At the same time, it creates a channel for the conversation that is flexible, yet goal-directed. This is how it differs from using similar communication behaviors when you do not have a goal in mind, where your intention may simply be to gather information or to assist another person in solving his or her own problem. As an influencer, you are consciously and openly moving toward a goal. You know that the other person has to go there with you willingly, so you make it easier for him or her to move in that direction.

Just as expressive behavior can be used in a way that disempowers others, receptive behaviors can be used in a manipulative way by someone acting as if he or she has no agenda, but behaving in a way that makes it clear that one exists (see Chapter 16). This is an ineffective and dishonest use of receptive behavior. It seldom works very well the first time, and it most certainly will not work a second time. As the saying goes, "Fool me once, shame on you—fool me twice, shame on me!"

Phrasing a statement as a question does not mean it will be perceived as receptive behavior. Others will experience questions that present a position or suggest that there is a right answer, as "tell" behaviors. For example, "What does your father always say about that?" is another way of saying, "You'd better do what Dad tells you to do." Questions that include the phrases, "Don't you think . . . " or "Do you agree . . . " are almost always expressive in nature. Leaders and managers are often surprised to learn that employees did not feel involved in a decision, even though they believed themselves to be inquiring and soliciting their ideas. This usually occurs when the subtext is a clear "tell" message. The right, or politically wise, answer was clear. We are very good, as a species, at figuring this out.

Because receptive guidance must be light, rather than heavy, in order to be effective, it is essential that the influencer adopt a neutral, nonjudgmental point of view. If questions and comments promote—even subtly—the influencer's point of view, they will be treated, correctly, as expressive statements. People sometimes misuse receptive influence behaviors in the hope that they will not be caught influencing (see Chapter 16) and that the other person will believe that the result was his or her idea. This virtually never works. Most people are sensitive to having "words put into their mouths" and will not be fooled or coerced into commitment. They may "go along to get along." Many managers mistake their direct reports' political expediency for evidence of their own leadership and influence.

Because of the nature of receptive influence, it is almost never a one-way process. In drawing out and learning about the other person, the influencer will adapt and adjust and develop new ideas—sometimes even changing the influence goal as a result of new information. Often, effective receptive influence behavior provides an opportunity for both participants to accomplish important goals.

The Receptive Behaviors

Receptive behaviors include inquire, listen, attune, and facilitate (Figure 5.1).

1. You can *inquire* by asking open-ended questions (ones that cannot be answered by "yes" or "no") and drawing the other person out.

   - "Where should we consider going on our vacation this year?" (Ask open-ended questions)

   - "You mentioned that you were not comfortable with the direction we are taking. Tell me more about what you are thinking." (Draw out)

2. You can *listen* by checking understanding and by testing implications of what the other has said.

   - "So from your point of view, that contractor has too little experience with custom-designed homes for you to feel comfortable." (Check understanding)

   - "I'm sensing that you're pretty hot under the collar about that." (Test implications)

Figure 5.1.   Receptive Influence Tactics and Behaviors

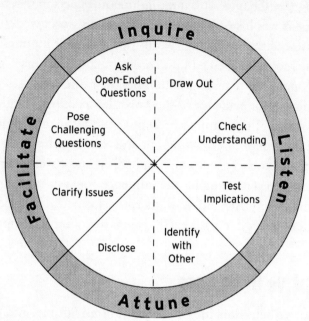

Exercising Influence, Revised Edition. Copyright © 2007 by John Wiley & Sons, Inc. Reproduced by permission of Pfeiffer, an Imprint of Wiley. www.pfeiffer.com

3. You can *attune* by identifying with the other person and disclosing information about yourself.

   • "If I were you, I might well be concerned about whether that would affect my eligibility." (Identify with other)

   • "I didn't listen to your ideas very well the last time we discussed this." (Disclose)

4. You can *facilitate* by clarifying issues and posing challenging questions.

   • "It seems that you are caught between wanting to be a good team player and feeling strongly that your idea is the only successful way to go." (Clarify issues)

   • "What would it take for you to be willing to put off the trip for a year?" (Pose challenging questions)

How Receptive Behaviors Work

- *Inquire* behaviors influence by establishing the topic, the issues, and the questions to be explored. In addition to providing information, they can encourage people to think along new lines, to consider new questions, and to deepen and expand their thinking about specific issues. This creates an opening for influence.

- *Listen* behaviors influence by clarifying, selecting, and emphasizing key areas of interest to both parties.

- *Attune* behaviors influence by creating an atmosphere of trust and common ground between the influencer and the other person. We are most likely to be influenced by people whom we trust.

- *Facilitate* behaviors influence by creating a bias toward action on the part of the other person. We are more likely to take action when someone we respect assumes we will, believes we can, and gives us just a slight push off the fence.

Nonverbal Components of Receptive Behaviors

Being receptive means attending to what the other is saying and doing. Nonverbal behaviors, such as making eye contact at key points when you ask a question or check your understanding (but not constantly or invasively), are useful. Gestures that are inclusive and inviting help the flow of conversation. Being sensitive to the rhythm of the other's speech and gestures and joining with it in a gentle way can help bring the two of you into harmony. Relaxed facial muscles allow you to respond in a natural way to the information that flows between you.

Sitting in a relaxed posture and inclining your head toward the other person communicates your interest. Arranging to sit kitty-corner rather than directly across from the other person indicates a conversational rather than a confrontational purpose for the discussion. Sitting or standing at the same level as the other is helpful, especially if you are seen as having legitimate power or authority over him or her by virtue of position, age, or other aspects of the relationship. For example, you will probably have a better influence conversation with a young child if you are sitting in a low chair.

The emotional and vocal tone that supports receptive behavior is relaxed, curious, and nonjudgmental. If there is an edge to your voice, the other person will probably shut down, assuming that he or she is probably in trouble with you. (If that is the case, it is better to express your point of view first, to put it on the table, or to disengage temporarily until you can use receptive behavior in a more nonjudgmental way.) Be especially careful to leave silence after you speak, to allow the other person time to think about and make a response. Don't step on his or her lines.

You shouldn't leave the other with the impression that you are uninterested or have nothing to say about a topic if that is not the case. You can be alert for nonverbal signs that he or she has completed a thought or gotten to the bottom of an issue so you will know when to interject an expressive comment. Notice, for example, when the other person drops his or her voice at the end of a sentence and adopts a more relaxed posture.

Using Receptive Influence at Work

The most obvious use of receptive influence at work is to obtain information that will help you guide others' thinking about issues. In most organizations, information is an important source of power, and significant data is not always readily available.

You can't get someone's help or shared commitment to a goal without knowing how the other person is thinking about the issue involved. You can't sell someone on an idea or proposal if you don't know his or her decision criteria. You can't negotiate a good and fair agreement with someone if you don't know what he or she wants or needs in relation to the subject at hand. You can't resolve conflicts unless you know how each party is interpreting the situation and what each feels is to be gained or lost.

- "What ideas do you have about the new exhibition booth?" (Ask open-ended questions)

- "So, your decision will be based primarily on whether the proposal helps us meet the customer's need for scalability." (Check understanding)

- "What would it take for you to commit to this schedule?" (Pose challenging questions)

- "If I were you, I might be worried about how this will affect my budget for next year." (Identify with others)

Receptive behaviors invite others to contribute and grow in confidence and skill. A young executive I once worked with had moved rather quickly from being an outstanding individual contributor to being the head of an important department. He prided himself on having excellent solutions to nearly every problem that his group had to deal with, and he shared them with his staff in the hope that they would learn from him. Yet his people were not developing in the way that he had hoped; he was growing impatient with their lack of imagination. After receiving some rather difficult feedback (as part of a coaching process), he realized that he was not in the habit of asking questions and listening to the ideas that his very talented people tentatively put forward. One day he made a memorable statement: "I am no longer in the business of being a star; now I have to create stars." He knew that "no great idea ever entered the mind through the mouth," and so he decided to use only receptive behaviors at his next staff meeting. To his surprise and delight, his staff was full of ideas—and very excited about having the chance to express them.

One of the mistakes leaders and others often make is to accept the first response, or presenting problem, as the real issue. Thus, we spend a lot of time solving the wrong problems or trying to solve problems that others need to handle. Receptive influence behaviors allow us to learn, in depth, what the real issues are while guiding others along a path toward shared responsibility and commitment.

- "You mentioned that you were a little uncomfortable with that deadline. Tell me more about that." (Draw out)

- "You look as if you are uncertain whether to commit to this course of action. Is that right?" (Test implications)

- "Here's why I'm asking. I'm nervous about the upcoming executive committee meeting and I want to feel totally prepared." (Disclose)

- "What options do you have for dealing with that problem?" (Pose challenging questions)

On teams, receptive influence is essential for getting members' involvement and thus their commitment and energy behind any course of action. Team members can build productive relationships quickly with one another across functional lines by using receptive influence.

- "What do you think we need to do to make this work for the customer?" (Ask open-ended questions)

- "Help me understand more about how you would like me to assist with that." (Draw out)

- "As I understand your situation, you want to work on this with me, but your dilemma is that you don't think your functional manager would support it." (Clarify issues)

- "What will it take for you to be able to commit to meeting this deadline?" (Pose challenging questions)

In today's competitive environment, one of the keys to organizational success is the ability to learn quickly and communicate that learning to others in the organization. Organizational learning has to happen through the individual use of receptive behaviors.

- "How did you get that proposal accepted so quickly by the customer's legal department? What worked?" (Ask open-ended questions)

- "So, it seems that your team has gone to a shared database solution." (Check understanding)

- "One thing I learned on this project is that I made a big mistake in over-engineering that kind of product; in the future I'll be more aware that the customer isn't likely to pay for that degree of perfection." (Disclose)

- "You mentioned that you wouldn't use that vendor again. I'd like to hear what your experience was." (Draw out)

Using Receptive Influence at Home

In your family or household, receptive influence helps you discover how members are feeling and involves them in decisions that will affect their lives in important ways. It is a means of expressing confidence and respect for others and, in this way, creates an atmosphere of mutual trust. Asking for and listening to others' ideas also invites them to be more open to your ideas. A very common complaint in families is, "He/she never listens to me." This is another way of saying, "I'm not respected around here. My opinions don't count."

Even young children can respond to and reciprocate with good influence behavior.

- "How do you think we should assign the housework tasks?" (Ask open-ended questions)

- "You've been very quiet all day. I'm wondering if you're worried about Pyewacket's visit to the veterinarian tomorrow?" (Test implications)

- "I shouldn't have yelled at you about breaking the dish. I know you didn't mean to do it." (Disclose)

- "So, you're sad that your teacher didn't choose you to go on the trip this time." (Check understanding) "What can you do to show her that you are ready for the next one?" (Pose challenging questions)

Children who are treated in this respectful manner are more likely to respond in a mature and productive way, regardless of age. On an outing with my then four-year-old grandson, I asked him to think about his behavior. "Isaac, why did you run away just then?"

He responded, "I forget to manage myself when I have chocolate ice cream."

"What do you think you can do about that?"

"I shouldn't ask for it."

"And what else could you do?"

"I could be the boss of me, even if I eat ice cream."

In potentially difficult or emotionally charged situations with adults and older children, it is especially important to lead with receptive behavior (using a nonjudgmental approach and tone of voice) before you find yourself in an attack-and-defend spiral. Doing this requires serious self-management, including knowing when and how to disengage if you begin to feel and act defensive.

- "Help me understand what I did that upset you just now." (Draw out)

- "So you waited because you expected me to pick you up as I did the last time?" (Check understanding)

- "If I were you, I would probably have felt angry and put down by what I said to you when I left this morning." (Identify with other)

- "So you were really disappointed with the way I was approaching the situation, but didn't want to embarrass me in front of the kids . . . is that right?" (Test implications)

Using Receptive Influence in Your Community

Many community issues bring out individuals and groups with a wide range of interests. A major task of leaders in community organizations is finding those interests that are common to all and that might hold promise of agreements or solutions. This can only be done by the judicious use of receptive behaviors.

Even large-scale meetings can be designed so that participants are invited and encouraged to listen to and learn from one another. (See the article on meeting design in Appendix C.)

- "What are the issues that bring each of you to this meeting?" (Ask open-ended questions)

- "Do I understand you to say that no one from your group has ever been part of the leadership of this organization?" (Check understanding)

- "You're right. I did cut that discussion short after I promised to hear everyone's views. Let's return to it." (Disclose)

- "What are some things we can do that will achieve our goal without going over the budget?" (Ask open-ended questions)

Perhaps the most important use of receptive behaviors in community settings is for the purpose of understanding widely differing points of view. This is far preferable to the common situation in communities when interest groups break down into ever-smaller cohorts with single-issue themes.

When to Use Receptive Behaviors

In summary, use receptive influence behaviors at work, at home, and in your community under the following circumstances:

- You need important information that is not self-evident

- You want the other person to be committed to the decision

- You want to get to the bottom of a problem

- You need the other person to take an action that you cannot take yourself

- You want to express respect for the other person and his or her opinions and ideas

- The other person has indicated, by repeating him- or herself or by withdrawing, that he or she does not feel listened to

- You intend to use the information that you receive in a way that the other person will agree is a benefit—or at least not harmful to him or her

A key to successful influence is the ability to balance expressive and receptive behaviors over time in an influence relationship. If I know that you are open to hearing my point of view, I'm much more willing to listen to yours. If I know that you are not just "picking my brain" (a graphic and unpleasant image), but are also willing to tell me what you know and think about the topic, I'll go a little further out on a limb to give you information and opinions.

CHAPTER 6

Influencing in Action

"The law of nature is, do the thing, and you shall have the power: but they who do not the thing have not the power."

—Ralph Waldo Emerson

Responding to Opportunities

There is no shortage of influence opportunities. You are limited only by time, energy, or expectations. These opportunities come in many forms. Sometimes they occur during formal or informal meetings. Sometimes they arise spontaneously over a meal or around the copier. For example, someone you would like to influence may offer you opportunities such as:

- A request for ideas or solutions

- A complaint about the status quo

- An expression of uncertainty or confusion

- A casual remark that touches on a subject of interest

We frequently ignore these opportunities—sometimes for good reasons and sometimes for bad reasons.

Some good reasons to turn down an opportunity to influence include:

- Your experience or intuition suggests that the person is not open to influence right now.

- The issue is not important enough to you to offset the effort or the risk that you anticipate would be involved.

- The timing is not right and you believe you would be more effective after a change in the situation (the other person's need becomes greater, you have an opportunity to get others' support, you can plan and practice an effective approach, etc.).

- You believe that you are not in a legitimate position to exercise influence on this issue with this person (for example, you might be perceived as using power because of your position or relationship; the situation calls for an expertise you do not have; etc.).

Some bad reasons to ignore an influence opportunity include:

- You would prefer to settle for the status quo, even though you are uncomfortable with it, rather than risk disapproval or failure.

- You tend to keep your expectations low, rather than try to improve your chances of acquiring what you want.

- You believe that good ideas should sell themselves or that if you are in the right you should succeed without having to make a special effort.

- You are inclined to take out your frustration with the status quo by complaining or blaming others, rather than by taking action yourself.

In my family and in my company, when an issue is in contention, it is understood by everyone that the person who cares the most about something generally gets to have it his or her way—and also must shoulder the responsibility for making it happen. Influence success often carries the burden of having your name on a lot of the items on the action list—and all over the outcome. So the choice of whether or how intensely to influence about something is always tempered by how important it is to you and by how much of your resources you're willing to spend on it. That, it seems to me, is how it should be—and it gives each of us a strong motivation to succeed, if only to prove that we were right. Even the ornery side of human nature can be put to good use.

Creating Opportunities

Sometimes the right influence opportunities don't present themselves, and you have to create them. The person you need to influence may not appear at the lunch table. The issue may not arise in casual conversation. Something that is of great importance to you may not be on anyone else's screen right now. Here are some ways to create those opportunities:

- Set up a formal meeting (in person, by telephone, or electronically) on the topic and invite the people you want to be there.

- Invite the person you want to influence for lunch or coffee and raise the issue directly. This can work well for people who are more extraverting and are comfortable with thinking out loud.

- Send an e-mail or phone message indicating that you would like to meet informally to discuss the issue. This is especially effective if the person is more introverting, someone who likes to think about a subject before discussing it.

- During a casual conversation, mention that you would like to discuss the issue with him or her. Ask whether this is a convenient time or, if not, make a date to do so.

Managing Influence Situations

The experience of managing influence situations may be a new one for you. It will require you to be thoughtful and tactical in the way you initiate and respond. In Part II of this book you will learn how to plan and prepare for an important influence situation. Still, much of the influencing you do will be in response to the kind of opportunities that suddenly present themselves or that you are able to create in the moment. Consider the suggestions in the following paragraph. Use them as you go about your life over the next few days. See what you can learn about influencing through some low-key experimentation. You will probably not change the world right away, but you will probably not start World War III either.

As opportunities arise, or as you can create them:

- Tell yourself what you hope will happen as a result.

   "I'd like to be assigned to that task force."

- Let the other person know what you are up to.

   "I'd like to get your ideas about how I might have more input on the project scope."

- Think about and present the situation from the other's point of view, not just your own.

   "If you can help me get the house ready, I'll be able to drive you to the mall in time to meet your friends."

- If the other person's reaction or response surprises you, use inquire and/or listen behaviors to understand it better.

   "So you weren't aware that I was expecting to be involved in the decision?"

- Maintain a balance of expressive and receptive behaviors. If you start by presenting an opinion or suggestion, continue by learning how the other person thinks or feels about the idea.

   "What do you think about it?" or "How does that strike you?"

- If the other person seems upset or reluctant to discuss the issue, disengage temporarily and let him or her know when you will reinitiate the discussion.

  "I can see that this isn't a good time for you to talk about this. How about if I call you early next week to set up a meeting?"

These are some ways to get started on the path of becoming conscious, tactical, and successful as an influencer. You will continue to learn through reading, observation, conscious practice and rehearsal, feedback, experimentation, and reflection. As with any fitness program, there is no graduation (but there are continuing opportunities to test yourself).

PART I

Exercising Influence

- Clarify and refine your goal.

- Highlight the most important issues related to relationship and context.

- Select the three or four most useful behaviors, using the criteria you will find in Chapter 14.

- Modify your choice of behaviors based on what you know about yourself as an influencer, as well as the fit with the culture and the individual.

- Develop some ways of expressing what you want to say at key points, framed so you will make sense to the other person.

Phase Three: Troubleshooting

Think about everything that could derail your plan. Do some "if . . . then" contingency planning. What will you do if the worst case occurs? Consider also the possibility that you may be wildly successful and may have aimed too low. How can you adjust your aspirations upward during the meeting? Think of some alternate sources of need satisfaction if this influence opportunity simply doesn't work out as you intended.

Of course, it is difficult to focus on the downside when you are trying to be optimistic. A certain amount of "magical thinking" may set in, leading you to ignore possibilities that you don't want to believe could happen. (Magical thinking is the process we use to ignore the elephant under the rug, thinking that if we don't acknowledge it, perhaps it will go away.) By remembering to take this step before you are in the situation, you will be prepared for most eventualities and less likely to be distracted from your goal by an unexpected response. The more important the situation, the more useful it is to consider multiple possible responses and plan how to deal with the ones that will have the most impact on your results.

CHAPTER 8

Establishing Influence Goals

"A good intention clothes itself with sudden power. When a god wishes to ride, any chip or pebble will bud and shoot out winged feet, and serve him for a horse."

—Ralph Waldo Emerson

If You Don't Know Where You're Going . . .

To paraphrase the Cheshire cat in *Alice in Wonderland,* if you don't know where you're going, any road will get you there. Often, the greatest distinction between the person who comes away from a meeting with a good result and the one who is disappointed is that the first person was clear about what he or she wanted before the meeting began. Being aware of your goal and consciously working toward achieving it takes time and energy, but is usually considerably more effective than improvisational advocacy. So . . . the first step in planning how you are going to influence another person or group is to frame a goal.

I have spent many difficult hours, both as a consultant and as a member of the organization, sitting in meetings and imagining what someone from another, more logical planet, might assume were the influence goals of the participants.

Judging from the behavior used (such as sarcasm, put-downs, and direct attacks), it might seem that they were trying to do some or all of the following:

- Get a colleague to admit that he or she was bad, wrong, or stupid

- After achieving that, get the same person to acknowledge the correctness or brilliance of the influencer and/or his or her idea and to agree

- Have a third party agree with the influencer on both counts

If asked, of course, the participants would probably say that their goal was to influence the others to agree with and implement a suggestion or proposal. However, they did not behave as if they were attempting to move the others in that direction—or else they would have noticed that everything they were doing was fixing the others more firmly in their own positions and increasing their resistance. Being clear in advance on what you hope to accomplish can help you avoid these meetings from hell and achieve the result that you really want. Making your underlying intentions conscious enables you to decide whether or not your current influence goal is one you really want to achieve.

Having a conscious goal is risky; it raises common human fears of failure and of alienating others who may see us as too aggressive. If we don't make a commitment to influence, we have the luxury of blaming others when we don't like the results of decisions that might have been within our sphere of influence. No amount of sophisticated understanding or practice of influence behaviors will make up for the reluctance to commit to an influence goal. Deciding that a result is unattainable before you give it a fair shot may create short-term comfort, but leads to longer-term disappointment in yourself and in your life.

You will learn the most from this section of the book by creating an influence plan for a situation you have identified as important to your own success and well-being. In Appendix B, you will find a template for a complete influence plan. I suggest that you try using the template or modifying it to include issues that are important to you and to exclude ones that seem irrelevant. Use it to plan for an important, upcoming influence opportunity at work, at home, or in your community. After you have implemented your plan, regardless of the outcome, make notes on what worked, what did not, and what you learned. This is a discipline that will help you to grow and improve as an influencer. Try to make new mistakes each time, rather than repeating the same old ones. If you never make any mistakes, you are probably not taking enough risk and not doing much influencing.

Developing a Challenging Influence Goal

Your influence goal provides the motivation to succeed . . . so it should be attractive enough to be worth the effort, yet achievable enough to keep you from giving up too easily. I remember a high school acquaintance who attempted to prove that God did not exist by praying that the Deity would cause a light switch to fly around the room (the word "sophomoric" has useful layers of meaning in this case). Someone else remarked that he assumed any self-respecting God would have better things to do with his or her time and that he assumed the would-be atheist did also. So it is with influence goals: they should be worthy both of your time and of the efforts of the being you are hoping to influence.

Influence goals are different from other goals that you set, in that they must be realized within a short and specific time frame. It won't help you to be a powerful influencer if you have to wait several weeks to see whether your behavior has achieved any results. You need to know at the time you are influencing whether what you are doing is moving you toward your goal. This will help you know whether and when you need to change or rethink your approach.

Your influence goal should be clear to you, not vague and amorphous. Ideally, it should be one that would be understood both by you and by the other party if you were to state it directly, using tell behaviors. "I would like to influence my teammate to use the new software program" is clearer than "I would like to influence him to upgrade."

Figure 8.1 is a useful set of criteria to test whether an influence goal will be effective. Rather than giving up on an influence result that may seem, at first, to be unattainable, use the criteria to sharpen and improve your goal. For convenience, they are summarized by the acronym, FOCUS.

Flexible

Being aware of the need that underlies your influence goal will enable you to be flexible and alert for opportunities. Through the use of receptive influence, you may become aware of alternative ways of meeting your needs that might be of more value to you or less difficult for the other person to provide. Knowing when to shift to an alternate means of need satisfaction ensures that you will have fewer failures as an influencer. Being flexible enables you to frame your goal in a way that has a realistic chance of leading you toward success. Your influence goal should be specific enough about ends to make sure your needs are met, while being flexible enough to allow for alternative means. Specificity refers to dates, times, amounts, and so forth, and ensures that you do not settle for something that does not go far enough toward meeting your needs. It gives you criteria to test whether or not an alternative result can work for you. An example of a goal that is both flexible enough and specific enough might be, "to have the vestry commit today to selecting the new minister by September 30." This goal leaves room for a variety of solutions about how the selection will be made, but is firm about when.

Figure 8.1.   Criteria for Influence Goals

- **F**lexible
- **O**bservable
- **C**ourageous
- **U**seful
- **S**upportive

Observable

Your influence goal should be designed so that you will be able to observe, during the influence opportunity, whether you are moving closer to it or further away. This will enable you to adjust or adapt your behavior appropriately. For example, the goal "to get my manager to change her mind about my project" is not observable. If, instead, you stated it, "to get my manager to make a commitment to funding my project," you would know whether you are moving closer to or further from the result you wish to achieve.

Courageous

Your influence goal should be optimistic—possible, but a stretch—so that the effort you put forth to achieve it will seem worthwhile to you. Attempting to achieve an important influence goal always requires a degree of risk, if only of disappointing yourself, and thus is an act of courage. "I want to influence my manager to commit $10K to do an exploratory project" is more courageous than "I want to influence my manager to agree to let me spend a day working on the proposal."

Useful

We sometimes set up influence goals that will not meet our most important needs. For example, "to have my spouse admit that he or she was wrong about the old contractor" would not be as useful as a goal that states: "to get my spouse's commitment to hire the new contractor I have found." It is helpful to question yourself about whether your influence goals meet short-term ego needs (which almost always will have a negative impact on the influence relationship) or will lead to longer-term, more important results. Of course, there are times when meeting the shorter-term need might really be more important to you, but with the recognition that you may go down with the ship you just sank. (A former husband used to ask me, "Do you want to be right, or do you want to get the result you want?" Sometimes I had to think about it for quite a while. . . .)

Make sure your goals are not only useful, but also optimistic enough to be worth pursuing.

Supportive

Although influence goals are short-term, they need to be aligned with longer-term strategic goals in order to be effective. If you align your influence goals with the larger goal you hope to achieve, you will avoid being at cross-purposes with yourself, your organization, or your family and thus minimize the resistance to your idea or suggestion. For example, if your long-term goal is to work abroad, you will want to make sure that you don't set an influence goal for your manager to assign you to a long-lasting project that will keep you close to the home office.

Testing your goal statement against some or all of these criteria will lead you to sharpen and improve it so that it becomes a powerful tool for influencing. An influence goal that meets these criteria can be ambitious and optimistic, yet realistic and attainable.

The Value of Persistence

Something that clearly distinguishes successful influencers and leaders from others is that they are persistent in the pursuit of their influence goals. They do not take "no" for an answer very easily. They tend to know when to back off (see Chapter 18) and wait for another opportunity or be sensitive to when they should change their approach and tactics and try again.

Persistence helps in several ways. First of all, you may have been mistaken or be missing some data in your original analysis of the framework for influence. Thus, your timing could be wrong or you might need to do some preliminary work on the relationship to prepare for another influence attempt. Giving up too easily does not allow you to explore these possibilities.

Secondly, the fact that you are persistent (without being inappropriately aggressive) lends power to your influence attempts. Caring about an issue deeply enough to continue to bring it to others' attention demonstrates the strength of your commitment. One member of my staff used to greet me with a cheerful, "I'm baaaack!" before he launched into another pitch for something he believed to be important. He knew that eventually his persistence would pay off, although he might have had to be flexible about his approach and about specifics such as timing and cost. He would often make several strategic retreats and try again before I was sufficiently worn down to agree—but his success rate was high, and I was not put off by his efforts.

CHAPTER 9

Focus on the Relationship

"Let us be poised, and wise, and our own. Let us treat the men and women well: treat them as if they were real, perhaps they are."

—Ralph Waldo Emerson

You, Me, and Us

During a previous marriage that was marked by an excessive amount of processing (from my point of view), I remember saying in exasperation, "It seems that there are always three of us to deal with here . . . you, me, and the relationship." In fact, we are different in each of our personal, business, and other influence relationships. Each of us has aspects of our culture, personality, talents, education, experience, associations, interests, and memories that connect in different ways with different people. In this way, each relationship is unique. Each person knows and connects to some aspects of me that would surprise another person. One friend sees me as goal-directed and organized; another experiences me as a flake. One direct report finds my lack of attention to detail rather charming, making room for her to grow, while another is constantly disappointed that I need a reminder from him if he wants my input by a specific date. I have a very different influence relationship with each of them.

Influence relationships don't have to be very close; you don't even have to like one another. But you do need to acknowledge that there is a value to the relationship, that mutual respect and support is important, that "one hand washes the other." You need to know that you can trust the other person to keep agreements, to respect confidentiality, to approach the relationship with the intention of being fair. You need to believe that you have enough vested interests in common that you will both want to maintain the balance in the relationship.

Understanding what makes a particular influence relationship unique will help make it successful. Knowing what values and goals you share and what is likely to create conflict means that you will less often be surprised or unprepared to influence (or be influenced by) this particular person.

The Importance of Balance

Overall, the most important thing to remember about influence relationships is that they only work well when they are kept in balance virtually all of the time. That means that neither party feels that he or she is always the target, rather than the initiator of influence. Both parties should have relatively equal expectations of gaining support from or influencing the decisions of the other.

One way to ensure that this is so is to make sure that you use both expressive and receptive behaviors whenever you influence, so there will always be an opening for the other to reciprocate. Another way is to have regular check-ins with the people who are the most important to your success. You can do this in a low-key way and be quite explicit with one another about what is working and what needs to change in your influence relationship. But it only works if you check in on a regular basis—not just when a relationship crisis looms.

Studying History Versus Being Condemned to Repeat It

Sometimes you choose the people with whom you will have an important influence relationship; often they choose you or are chosen for you. In all cases, it is important to remember that the past creates the future. Before you begin to influence in a new relationship, find out something about what the person might be expecting from you. These expectations might be based on past history with your organization, profession, or department, other people in your role, or past experiences with you that you may not recall (or with someone like you). Using receptive behavior to learn about preferred norms or processes (how he or she would like to work together on this), as well as any concerns or preferences he or she might have, can get the relationship off to a good start.

If you are surprised by the other person's reaction to your influence behavior, stop the process and ask about it or, if that is inappropriate, disengage temporarily and ask someone who is in a position to know what the problem might be. If you learn about a past problem that is creating concern or wariness in the present, avoid any tendency to become defensive or to try to justify the past. Instead, use this as a learning opportunity; use receptive behavior to find out all you can about it. If necessary, disclose and acknowledge your part in or your organization's contribution to any issues that may get in the way of the current influence opportunity. Use expressive behavior to let the other person know where you stand and what you hope to achieve by working together.

Creating Your Influence Future

Each time you influence someone, you are making it easier or more difficult to influence him or her in the future. A successful and balanced outcome will motivate both of you to repeat the process, building a longer-term and more effective relationship.

If you plan to be part of an organization or industry or profession for the long run, there is no time like the present to build new and strong influence relationships. The very person you write off or treat disrespectfully today may be in a position to give or withhold support for something important to you tomorrow.

Some ways you can build influence relationships for the future include:

- Fix anything that is broken in a current influence relationship, and do it at a time when you are not seeking to influence that person.

- Seek out people with interesting ideas and learn more about them.

- Ask people you respect but don't know well to help you on a task or project.

- Offer to help someone whom you would like to get to know better on a task or project.

- Give public credit to people whose ideas you like and use.

- Invite a new person to join a task force or participate in a "think tank" meeting.

- Take time to congratulate a co-worker on a job well done.

Over time, your influence relationships will become a rich source of ideas, information, referrals, and mutual support. These people will be your coalition partners, champion your ideas, recommend you for that promotion, write blurbs for the cover of your book, hire your children as summer interns, and stand up and be counted when you need them. You don't have to take them out to dinner, but it wouldn't hurt to do lunch once in a while.

CHAPTER 10

Focus on the Context

The Individual

"All persons are puzzles until at last we find in some word or act the key to the man, to the woman; straightway all their past words and actions lie in light before us."

—Ralph Waldo Emerson

Influence Happens in the Other Person

Annoying, but there it is. No matter how well you have convinced yourself that your idea is the best thing since postable notes, if the other person doesn't buy it, you haven't influenced. It would be a perfect (albeit boring) world if everyone thought like you do; since they don't, you have to know as much as possible about the person you need to influence.

I once had a client who was the senior vice president of engineering in a large public utility. He was working on being more effective with the executive committee. I asked him to tell me how he usually approached them when he wanted funding for a project. He explained how carefully he put together the proposals with an emphasis on important structural engineering details as well as costs. Unfortunately for him, nearly all the members of the executive committee were attorneys or accountants and were primarily interested in safety issues and what their exposure might be to lawsuits. The details of the design were not reassuring to them. They were not impressed with, and thus not influenced by, his proposals because their questions and concerns were not addressed. It was a big "aha" for him to realize that he should find out what their decision criteria were and let them be his guide, rather than share data that was convincing to him.

Understanding Values, Needs, and Aspirations

Three important things to understand about the person you wish to influence (and about yourself) in relation to your influence goal are

- *Values:* What does he or she believe should happen?
- *Needs:* What does he or she need or want to happen?
- *Aspirations:* What does he or she hope will happen?

The first question concerns values. Values usually come from one's culture, family, or profession. They are beliefs about what is right, true, and good; we use them as the basis for important decisions. An example would be, "I believe that everyone should be consulted on issues that will affect them directly." Needs have to do with current vested interests—what she or he has to gain or lose related to the issue at hand. An example is, "I need to have input on the reorganization of my project team." The third question has to do with longer-term aspirations, hopes, and dreams, for example, "I want to be involved in this decision in order to gain valuable leadership experience."

An important influence issue may involve any or all of these. Some issues are more value-based ("What should be included in our code of conduct?"). Some stimulate questions of vested interests ("Which project will we fund, and who will lead it?"). Some are related to important aspirations ("Where should I go to school?").

Suppose, for example, that you want to persuade your neighbor to help you initiate a community garden project. He or she may value the idea of neighborhood cooperation, or on the other hand, be a strong proponent of individual family privacy. Perhaps your neighbor has a strong need for a say in neighborhood esthetic decisions—or perhaps he or she has a demanding job and needs weekends and evenings to be available to his or her family. Does he or she hope to be a community leader or aspire to move to a more upscale neighborhood? Understanding the values, needs, and aspirations of your neighbor can help you choose a realistic, wise approach to influencing him or her on this issue. Understanding values, needs, and aspirations can, in some cases, lead you to modify your goal or decide to seek support elsewhere.

To learn a great deal about another person's values, needs, and aspirations, you only need to look and listen. Look at what is on display in his or her office or private space. Listen to the words, phrases, and themes that are emphasized over and over again in casual conversation and in meetings. Pay attention to what the person responds to favorably and his or her "hot buttons." You need not be secretive about it—we all like to discuss these things and usually prefer that the people we live and work with closely understand and respect our preferences.

It is essential to know that you cannot change anyone's values, needs, or aspirations through direct influence. You can expose others to alternative options and ideas, but you will have to stay out of their way while they deal with any internal changes they might choose to make. (This is particularly difficult when we are influencing family members or friends.) You can, however, keep their values, needs, and aspirations in mind as you influence them to take certain actions. If you can find an honest way to frame what you want them to do that is consonant with their values, needs, or aspirations, most of your work will be done for you. And you will have treated the person with respect. For example, a school counselor I once knew wanted to influence her principal not to suspend a boy with whom she was working. The child had gradually improved his behavior during the year as a result of a lot of hard work on her part, as well as his. She believed that, with a sustained effort, he would turn around, and that a suspension would interrupt the progress that was being made, especially since attendance was an issue for him. That morning, however, he had disrupted a class and the principal wanted to teach him a lesson. The principal was an ex-military officer who believed in a strictly enforced disciplinary code. The counselor knew that approaching him with a plea for leniency or anything he might read as excusing the boy's behavior would be useless. Instead, she stated, "I know how important it is to you that children be held responsible for their actions. I believe that we should not give him the 'out' of suspending him, but rather insist that he deal directly with the teacher and make an agreement with her to do something that will make up for the problems he caused." This was a realistic and honest alternative way of assessing the situation and presenting the case. It made good sense from the point of view of the principal. He accepted the suggestion.

If you understand these fundamentals, you can think your way into the other's mind and predict how he or she might respond to a specific influence issue. This will help you to prepare. For example, you can show him how the action you are hoping to stimulate will fit within his values. You can demonstrate to her how doing this will meet her needs. You can show how your aspirations are aligned around this issue. This is often called "reframing," and it is a powerful technique (see Chapter 14).

Working with Personality, Interests, and Preferences

There are many ways of classifying personality and preference. Some of them are well-researched, self-report instruments, such as the Myers-Briggs Type Indicator[4]; others are based more on your own intuition and observation. Anything that helps you understand which approaches usually work well or usually fail with a specific person will contribute to your success as an influencer. If you always approach other people in the way you prefer to be approached, you will likely be successful primarily with those who are most like you. This is a limitation most of us don't have the luxury of accepting.

Although it may seem surprising, most people are more than happy to let you know how to be successful in influencing them. In our Exercising Influence seminar, participants bring to class with

them assessments from five or six colleagues. Although some participants express concern because the forms are not anonymous (since
influence is very specific to particular relationships, anonymous
feedback would not be very useful), few people have trouble getting
important people in their lives to fill them out. Many people welcome
the opportunity to tell their managers, peers, or key subordinates
how to be more successful in influencing them! Participants often
ask someone from their households or friends to fill one out as well.
They are instructed to follow up in a way that will enable them to
discuss in an open and productive way what the other would like
them to do more of, less of, or differently.

In the Self-Study Guide,[5] there is a short version of this assess-
ment. You can fill it out on yourself, ask someone else to do it, or
imagine what someone you need to influence might tell you about
what you could do more of, less of, or differently. Once someone has
let you know what works best, there is a certain tendency for him or
her to show you that the recommended approach works. This can
contribute significantly to your success, to both persons' benefit.

All of this will help when you come to choose the influence
behaviors that will help you reach your goal with this person. Once
you understand what works well with someone, you don't have to
use only that behavior. It may not be the right tool for the job you
have to do. But you might want to use that behavior to set yourself
up for success, to create rapport or a comfort zone between you and
the other person. For example, with someone who values your friendship and is open in expressing feelings, you might want to begin
influencing with an honest disclosure. "Sam, I am uncomfortable in
asking you to do one more thing on this project. I have had to come
to you so many times in the past month." With someone who is more
analytical, you could begin with a summary of why you need him or
her to help you. In both cases, you will probably use negotiate behaviors to do the real influence work, but you have opened the discussion
by using an approach that respects the other person's preferences. In
addition, you will probably avoid using a behavior that drives the
other person up the wall (yes, some people are allergic to your beau-
tifully crafted rationales . . . or visions . . . or questions) and use one
that will do the job almost as well.

It is always useful to keep in mind any vested interests that the other may have. Be sure you are not asking the other to go against those interests, and, if you can, find a way to align your interests with those of the other person. See whether you can meet some need in a way that is legitimate and fair, given what you are asking of him or her. Seek to understand any problems that might be created if the person does what you ask and find a way to make it easier for him or her to say "yes." Finding common ground between you and the other person—something you both have to gain by your success—is often a key prerequisite to successful influencing in difficult situations.

Examining Your Assumptions

Most of what we think we know about other people is not tested. We see or hear something they say or do and immediately explain it to ourselves. We categorize it (limited, of course, by our previous experience or the book we just finished). If someone is important for you to influence, try noticing how you are explaining that person to yourself. ("She didn't stop by my desk this morning. She must be angry with me. Or maybe she noticed that I didn't include her in the conference invitation." "He's a sales guy; he won't want a detailed report.") Then, during the next few times you see that person, just notice what he or she does without making assumptions. Consider a variety of alternate explanations that fit the same facts. Then, before you have an important influence opportunity with this person, use your receptive behavior to learn something new about him or her. Find out, for example, how she or he likes to go about making decisions; what kind of information is helpful; how the person prefers to be influenced.

Assumptions make life easier; they also limit our freedom to experiment. Untested assumptions about the person we intend to influence can lead us down a fruitless path. We keep waiting for the person to behave in the expected way. When he or she doesn't, we become confused or angry. Or we avoid opportunities to influence, assuming that the other will not be open to change. A more constructive approach is to notice and question your assumptions about the person. Say, "What would I do if I didn't believe that?" Then do it.

Difficult People or Difficult Situations?

You've tried everything. You've been rational. You've been sensitive. You've been generous. You've been tough. Nothing has worked. Where, you ask, is the section on dealing with difficult people?

There isn't one. There isn't room for one. Because everyone is difficult for somebody, sometimes. Even you. Saying that someone is too difficult to deal with means the same thing as saying you have given up on influencing that person. Of course, you might want to do that . . . but if the issue is important enough, you won't. Instead, you will do your homework, find someone who can help you understand this person, examine your assumptions, try a different approach, do something that seems completely insane, vary your timing, or use some indirect influence.

And if that doesn't work, take the day off, and then figure out another way to get what you need. As George Herbert said in 1670 or so, "Living well is the best revenge." (I know, I always thought it was Dorothy Parker, too.)

CHAPTER 11

Focus on the Context

System, Organization, Culture, and Timing

"Every moment instructs, and every object: for wisdom is infused into every form."

—Ralph Waldo Emerson

Influencing in an Open System

It's all very well to know everything you can about the person you are going to influence and the issue you are going to influence about. You can even be exceptionally good at the influence behaviors you have decided to use and still end up without the result you hoped for—or with one that makes your worst case scenario look like a tea party.

Often that is because you have left a few important things out of your analysis, and they turned out to be the most important ingredients. It's as if your great-aunt Jane gave you the recipe for her famous chocolate cake, but just happened to leave out one or two items, and the cake turned out flat and tasted like chalk.

The reason that so many good influence intentions come to naught is that you are almost never dealing with a tabula rasa—a blank slate—a situation completely divorced from other realities.

The slate has been written on. Every influence opportunity is part of a larger, open system that involves a variety of other issues, people, organizations, cultures, and other things, tangible or intangible, that exist in or out of time and space. Any one of them can override your best plans or make your needs irrelevant. An "open system" is one that receives information from outside of itself (inputs), transforms it, and sends information back out (outputs). This is a good description of the organizations we work in and the families we are a part of. Many of the elements that enter an open system are outside of your sphere of influence, but should affect the way you choose to approach the influence opportunity. For example, you may wish to influence a senior manager to make a commitment to an important project. You have planned your approach for some time and have aligned it with the strategic business goals of the company. You have just learned that a large firm from another country has acquired the company. You must assume that the strategic business goals have changed. This will affect the way you approach the manager.

Since you are not going to be able to control, influence, or even know about all the important inputs to the system, the only defense is to ask yourself a few questions about absolutely anything that could derail or, for that matter, enhance your attempt to influence. You need to begin by scanning the system for what could cause problems or help you, and then "debugging" or adjusting your approach to take these issues into account. Usually you'll find that there are some current and compelling issues related to the person you are trying to influence, such as competing priorities and deadlines. Maybe there are other people who are important to the person's decision and who have an issue with you or your idea. There will be some bugs within the organization if one is involved, such as "hot buttons" (words, concepts, or ideas that stimulate a strong reaction because of historical associations), major initiatives, or competitive pressures. There may be some industry or cultural imperatives that you can't ignore. And, of course, there may be trends and issues in the world surrounding the system that can promote or prevent your idea from receiving a fair hearing at this time.

In Appendix B, you'll find a list of questions that will help you explore the system you are working within so that you can take advantage of opportunities or deal with problems as part of your influence planning process. By using them, you can create a better fit between your idea or proposal and the system within which you are influencing.

Organizations, Teams, and Families

Every human organization has its own current issues and priorities, its own way of operating, its own structure and politics. For example, in my family of origin, issues that were emotional were dealt with when my father was out of town; he did not enjoy conflict. My brother and I soon learned that if we brought up a contentious issue (that he and I agreed about) when Dad was around, we would often end up with a better deal from our more peace-loving parent than if we left it for our mother to settle with us. Knowing how the power structure works is useful. Equally important is an understanding of the current strategy, goals, and priorities. It is far easier to sell an idea that is aligned with those goals and priorities than one that is tangential.

To develop a better fit between your idea and the organization, focus first on where the organization is expending the most energy. If you can communicate how your idea solves a key organizational problem, supports important priorities, or speeds the way to achieving an important goal, you have a much better chance of success. Next, review the organization's structures and processes to make sure that you develop an approach that aligns with the way the organization (or team, or family) works. Study the norms or ground rules that suggest who to approach, and how and when to approach him or her. For example, my company sells training and development services. In some organizations, we are more successful when we deal with senior leaders directly. In others, we enter through the Human Resources or Organization Development groups, because they are in a strategic role and, as our colleagues, want to be in the loop.

Culture Is Context

Just as we assume that the fish has no concept of water, we seldom think about culture. It's just there—unless, of course, we find ourselves in one that is different from our own. And even then it takes work to realize that the Italians are not driving like that just to annoy you and the Japanese are not deliberately dragging out the preliminaries to the negotiation in order to wear you down. Culture can be national, regional, ethnic, or organizational. Professions and industries have cultures; even families, departments, and teams develop a set of norms, values, rituals, and taboos that can be seen as cultures. Cultural practices drive a great deal of behavior that is below our awareness and easy for others to misinterpret.

The ability to recognize when behavior is cultural rather than tactical (deliberately chosen to achieve a goal) is very useful to the influencer in reading the situation. Understanding the cultural context also helps you shape your influence approach in a way that will be a better fit for the person or group you are influencing. For example, the culture of a research and development organization is likely to be one in which expertise and reputation are highly valued. You would be well-advised to brush up on your chemistry or physics or (preferably) bring along someone whom the other person respects professionally if your influence opportunity involves anything remotely technical.

Timing Is Everything—Almost

Knowing what to do is one thing, and knowing when to do it is another. Once we have decided to take on an influence task and have prepared for it, it can be difficult to stop and wait. But timing has to be part of your recipe for success. There are times when moving on something quickly before the other person has too many options to deal with is the right thing to do. Sometimes it makes sense to wait until there are fewer demands on his or her attention or for a time when the issue is on his or her screen. Often, you will want to carry out your plan in stages. Nothing works all the time, but a well-thought-out plan considers timing as well as approach.

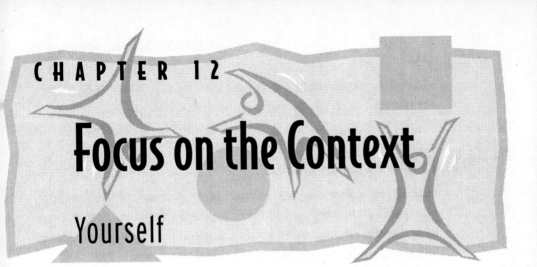

CHAPTER 12

Focus on the Context

Yourself

"Insist on yourself, never imitate."

—Ralph Waldo Emerson

Wants Versus Needs

At its core, influence is about getting what you want. Even though what you want may be to save the world or at least some small part of it, your goal is still more about you than about the world. So it's best to be very up-front with yourself about what it is that you want and what underlying needs or vested interests getting it would serve. A simple way to do that is to revisit your goal and ask yourself what it represents for you. Asking, "What would achieving this goal do for me?" is a simple way to get at your own motivations for influence. Sometimes by doing so we are clarified and strengthened in our commitment. Sometimes we realize that it is all about ego gratification and, in fact, a facelift or a new sports car would be cheaper. If you are not completely honest with yourself, you could find that getting what you tell yourself you want will not satisfy your underlying need. Honesty with yourself also has the bracing effect of helping you modify unrealistic influence goals, such as making your teenager admit that you are right about his or her hair. (Influencing him or her change the hairdo would be a more realistic goal.)

Strengths and Limitations

Having made a tentative commitment to go ahead and influence, you might as well review how hard you will have to work at it. If you have decided to do something that plays to your strengths (expertise, behavioral skill, reputation, comfort in a relationship), you will probably go ahead right away (if the timing is right). If not—if you have to work with a person with whom you have had tremendous conflict, or use a behavior that is very difficult for you to do with a straight face, or speak knowledgeably about a subject that you nearly flunked in elementary school—consider your options. Perhaps you need more time to prepare and a friend to rehearse with. Maybe you need to find someone to go with you or instead of you (see Chapter 18 on indirect influence). Perhaps you just need to alter your plan off the ideal course enough so that it fits you better.

Style and Blind Spots

Knowing yourself as an influencer can sometimes keep you out of trouble. Do you prefer or need time to think before you speak, or do you do best when you can respond in the moment? Do you like a lot of structure and preparation, or do you prefer to go in with a broad-brush approach? Do you enjoy taking risks by suggesting new ideas, or do you prefer to come in with a well-documented case? Do you enjoy David and Goliath moments (where you play David), or do you try to gain a balance of power before you go in?

Knowing what you prefer as an influencer does not mean that you can—or should—do it your way. In fact, understanding it may keep you from doing it your way when that style would not be appropriate to the situation. Comfort is not one of the common components of influencing. You will need to be wide awake and manage yourself. Blind spots are only blinding when you keep yourself unaware of them.

Think about any personal issues you have that are specific to this situation. Are you carrying any baggage about this person that could get in the way of being an effective influencer? Do you have any unfinished business or hidden agenda that you are aware of? If so, think of a way to settle it or set it aside before this influence opportunity. It will interfere with your effectiveness.

Keeping It Light

Nothing will drag you down as an influencer more than your awareness of the heaviness of your responsibility and the serious nature of what you are taking on. The natural fear of failure that we all have will expand, like any clutter, to fit the space available to it. The more important the influence attempt, and the more seriously you take yourself as an influencer, the more likely you are to slip on a banana peel, like the policemen in old silent films. There is a paradox about this business of influence. When we treat it as a sort of "theater game" of skill and chance, where we can move forward and back and sideways and up and down, and maybe have the other players get tangled up in unpredictable ways, we may prevail. When we treat it as a life-and-death drama starring ourselves as the heroes—well, after all those hours spent just in putting on the makeup, it's hard to improvise. Influence is nothing if not improvisational theater. Keep some corner of your mind available to be amused at your own antics and you will always have enough objectivity to allow yourself to take advantage of subtle shifts in the situation.

Readiness, Reluctance, and Risk

Influencing takes energy. (It can also be very energizing.) You will need to decide which goals are worth your effort. Sometimes you will influence to achieve a goal that is personally meaningful to you. Sometimes others will ask or tell you to be influential about something that you don't care about very much—or even something you don't agree with. Sometimes you will be daunted by an important or difficult influence opportunity. Sometimes the opportunity may seem too trivial to bother with. Knowing yourself as an influencer requires you to be ruthlessly honest about your commitment to achieving an influence goal. If you are not committed, you are unlikely to succeed. Most influence goals that are really worth achieving require some risk-taking on the part of the influencer. You will have to take a stand about something that may be unusual, innovative, even unpopular. You may need to communicate with people who have more power than you do or who have the ability to influence your career or your personal well-being for good or ill. You may be a person who prefers to avoid conflict and controversy. Influential people are visible, and the attention you attract may not always be to your liking. Balancing the strength of your commitment with the level of risk you are willing to take to achieve your goal will give you a realistic sense of your readiness to respond to an influence opportunity. If the risk seems too high, you can explore indirect influence options, take other steps to reduce the risk level, or let go of the goal. Any of those options is preferable to making a half-hearted attempt to influence. You won't get the results you want, and you will probably reduce your effectiveness and confidence as an influencer.

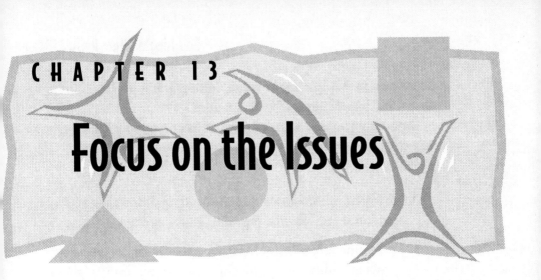

CHAPTER 13

Focus on the Issues

"A foolish consistency is the hobgoblin of little minds . . . "
—Ralph Waldo Emerson

Doing Your Homework

That's it, basically. If you have something important to influence
about, learn everything you can about it. Read everything you can
find, talk to everyone who knows more about it than you do. Don't
limit yourself by looking only for support or justification of your
point of view. Get familiar with all the counter-arguments and all
the potential threats that are related to your idea—all the needs and
fears that might arise for someone who actually had to agree to take
action on it. Think yourself into the mind of someone who would
be unalterably opposed to doing what you want done and then see
what it would take to change your mind, even to warm up to the
idea just a little.

Develop a list of benefits and costs for taking action—not just
for you (although that will be useful), but for the person or group
you hope to influence. Do a risk analysis. Identify what could go
wrong and how such problems could be prevented or mitigated.

Be sure to do this from your target person's point of view. Think about the risks of not taking action at all.

Anything you can do to stimulate dissatisfaction with the status quo may help move your idea forward. Some ways to do that include:

- Showing objective data that indicates problems with the current approach (decreasing sales figures, plunging grades, etc.)

- Providing information from third parties about needs or problems with the current situation (letters from neighbors, customer complaints, etc.)

- Finding benchmark examples of successful implementation of an idea or approach similar to the one you support

- Planning an evaluation with the group, team, or family to test what is and is not working about the present situation

Influencing people generally means getting them to change or modify the way they think, feel, or act. Behavioral scientists, such as the late Richard Beckhard, Ph.D., of the Sloan School of Management at MIT[6], have suggested that change occurs under the following conditions:

- There is sufficient dissatisfaction with the present state, and

- A positive vision of the future possibility, and

- Support for getting from the present to the ideal future state

Each of these must exist in sufficient strength to balance the perceived risks of change. The information you gather about the issue can serve to strengthen the other person's understanding in any of these areas.

When you have gathered the information, consider how best to present it to the person you want to influence. This kind of information is often most effective when the other person has a chance to absorb it on his or her own before you discuss it. You will also want to think about choosing information that focuses on the merits of your idea, rather than criticizing the status quo or viewpoint of the person you want to influence. It's best if you let the other person do that. It is easier to get someone to think about your idea as another, more useful alternative than to escape unscathed from someone who is fiercely defending his or her previous choices and decisions.

Even with all the homework you are doing, it is possible that you will persuade someone to agree that the situation needs to change, without deciding that your preferred solution or idea is the way to go. Consider possible alternatives and how close they would come to meeting your need or achieving your goal. You may have to shift to an alternative if it looks as if you will not achieve your original goal. Having already considered alternatives gives you some useful flexibility.

Confidence Is Power

The best thing about doing your homework is that it gives you confidence . . . Confidence that you know what you are talking about . . . Confidence that you are prepared to deal with questions and objections. Confidence has a very attractive quality: it lets the other person know that he or she can trust you on the issue. That is, unless you use your confidence in a manipulative way, by asking "trap questions" or otherwise putting down the other's position. Having confidence enables you to build up your position without tearing down that of the other. That way, you will not have to deal with defensive and self-protective resistance to your ideas.

CHAPTER 14

Choosing and Using Influence Behaviors to Achieve Your Goal

"A beautiful behavior is better than a beautiful form; it gives a higher pleasure than statues or pictures; it is the finest of the fine arts."

—Ralph Waldo Emerson

Reviewing the Influence Framework

During the preliminary influence planning process, you have set your goal and thought about the person you are influencing and your influence relationship. You have explored other factors in the context in which you will be influencing. All of this information will help you choose the behavioral tools or tactics that will help you achieve your goal. (I know the word "tactics" sounds military, but in this sense it just means the behaviors you consciously choose and use to move toward the result you want to accomplish.)

Look over the notes you have made and highlight the things that seem especially significant to this influence opportunity. In general, the more important the influence opportunity, the more elements you will take the time to consider. Now you are ready to develop a plan of action.

Selecting the Most Useful Behaviors

Tables 14.1 and 14.2 show criteria for selecting behaviors that will be most effective in your situation. You have probably already made a preliminary choice. In many cases, you will simply confirm this. However, the criteria will enable you to notice where context issues could make a particular behavior less effective than you would like. In that case, you can either select another behavior or, if there really is no practical alternative, you can do something to change the context. For example, if the situation requires that you make a suggestion about something when the other does not believe you to be an expert, you will probably want to enlist a person who is respected in that field to work with you.

Once you have decided on three or four behaviors, use the "sentence starters" in Appendix D to develop some ways to use them. You will not be reading from a script during the real event, but this practice will enable you to become more comfortable with the behaviors, especially if they are not the ones you use most often.

Reframing

One of the most important things you can do to prepare yourself to influence is to use what you know about the person and the organization to reframe your ideas in a way that will make sense within his or her model of the world. Earlier, we discussed the importance of understanding the values, needs, and aspirations of the other person. Once you do, you are in a position to take an idea that is important to you and frame it so that the other person can understand and see the value of it. This does not mean being dishonest about it; there are usually many different ways of looking at the same set of data.

You will need to look at the issue through the other person's frame if you are to be influential. For example, as a parent, you may want to influence your child's teacher to provide more individual attention and challenging assignments, rather than punishing him for misbehavior that you know comes from boredom. You know that she sees herself and wants to be seen as a supportive and helpful

Table 14.1. Guidelines for Choosing Expressive Behaviors

Use Tell behaviors when	Use Sell behaviors when
• The other is uncommitted on the issue	• The issue is open to different ideas, solutions, and interpretations
• You have a clear direction you want to take	• You can be relatively objective
• Choose Suggest when the other has defined the issue as a problem and you are seen as an expert	• Choose Offer Reasons when you are seen as an expert on the issue
• Choose Express Needs when the other would see your need as legitimate	• Choose Refer to Shared Values and Goals when you are seen as a partner
Do not use if the action would be against the other's interests	*Do not use* if you are not open to influence on the issue

Use Enlist behaviors when	Use Negotiate behaviors when
• You are on the same "team"	• Vested interests are involved
• The other is hesitant to take action	• The other perceives you as fair
• Choose Encourage when the other respects you and you are willing to offer help and support	• Choose Offer Incentives when you have tangible or intangible resources to exchange
• Choose Envision when you want to align and motivate	• Choose Describe Consequences when the other needs to know about them in order to make a good choice
Do not use if you are not genuinely enthusiastic	*Do not use* if you are unwilling to deliver on them

Table 14.2.   Guidelines for Choosing Receptive Behaviors

Use Inquire behaviors when	Use Listen behaviors when
• The other wants to be consulted or involved • You are genuinely interested in what he or she has to say	• The other believes you have a right to know • The other believes you can identify with his/her concerns
• Choose Ask Open-Ended Questions when you are opening a new topic • Choose Draw Out when you want to go deeper	• Choose Check Understanding when the information is relatively straightforward • Choose Test Implications when you want to deepen your understanding
Do not use if the other does not trust you	*Do not use* if you feel hostile toward the other

Use Attune behaviors when	Use Facilitate behaviors when
• You would like to create more openness • The other has a need for allies	• The other is accountable for taking action • The other would not lose face by accepting assistance from you
• Choose Identify with Other when the other already trusts you • Choose Disclose when you are willing to make yourself somewhat vulnerable in exchange for more openness	• Choose Clarify Issues when the other seems to be "stuck" • Choose Pose Challenging Questions when the other needs a stimulus toward action
Do not use if you do not trust how the other would use the information	*Do not use* if you have a specific action in mind

person. Rather than telling her what you think she is doing wrong, you might mention how much pleasure your son received from the time she spent with him, working on a special art project (Encourage).

Planning Your Approach

The most useful parts of your approach to plan in some detail are

- The first few minutes of the meeting or conversation: How will you start?

- Key transition points: How will you introduce or handle difficult issues?

- Conclusion: How will you move toward closure?

Remember, this will not be a play in which you and the other person have blocked the action and rehearsed your lines. It will be improvisational theater, and things will happen that you don't expect. Planning will help you anticipate and respond to these events only if you prepare for that possibility, so put some "what-ifs" in your plan. Troubleshoot it. Think about the worst case and what you might do if it happens. Think about what might signal you that things are going off course. Then decide what to do if this should occur. For example, what if your influence target becomes angry? What if he or she presents you with a major piece of information that is a complete surprise? Consider what could trigger a decision to set your goal aside while you use receptive behavior to probe for information. Under what conditions might you disengage? Consider the possibility that you might succeed sooner than you expected to. Is there a way you can build on that to accomplish other influence goals while you are on a roll, or should you end the meeting early and hope the other person doesn't feel that he or she has been a pushover?

Setting Yourself Up for Success

You can do a few things before you begin actively influencing the other person that will help you be successful. They may include:

- Resolve old issues that may get in the way of working on new ones.

- Garner the support of people who are respected by the other.

- Choose a time when the other person will be most likely to be receptive (after a milestone has been achieved, during a time of day when he or she will not be distracted, etc.).

- Choose a place where the two of you can talk (actually or virtually) without interruptions or fear of arousing apprehension on the part of others.

- Let the other person know your motivation and intentions for the meeting.

- Do anything else you can think of that will put the other person at ease about the meeting, such as sending a detailed agenda or including someone he or she trusts in the invitation.

- Begin the meeting by expressing optimism about the results.

- Take time to do a "check-in" before you get down to business (ask what is going on for the other person, whether he or she has anything to put on the agenda, etc.).

- Use behaviors that the other is most comfortable with to establish rapport at the beginning, even though your plan calls for you to use other behaviors to achieve your influence goal.

By taking some of these actions, you are not just trusting to luck or the other's good mood, but actively creating the conditions that give your plan the best possible chance for a successful outcome.

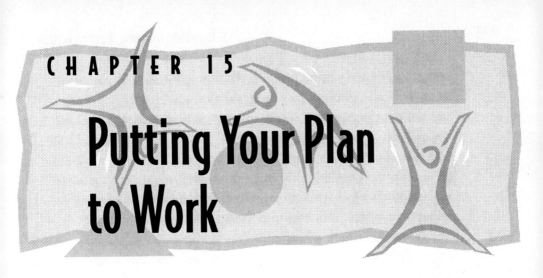

Putting Your Plan to Work

"The one thing in the world of value is the active soul."

—Ralph Waldo Emerson

Improvisation

If practicing influence skills is like participating in a fitness program
and planning for influence is like preparing for a journey, carrying
out an influence plan is a lot like doing improvisational theater.
You go in with a goal, some ideas about how to reach it, and a lot
of knowledge about the situation. There is no script, however, and
you are not the only actor. You have to respond to the lines the other
players feed you and to the developing situation without losing track
of where you want the performance to go. You have to be fast on
your feet and flexible in your approach.

Responding to New Information

No matter how carefully you plan, something will happen that you
didn't expect. Influence is a dynamic process, and it isn't a monologue—
there are other players. The approach that sounded great to your

spouse may leave your manager cold. The rationale that you developed for your customer may be irrelevant, now that he has spoken to your competitor. Your teenage daughter may have obtained her counselor's support for her "sabbatical" idea. What do you do now?

Probably the best piece of advice I have ever received on the subject is also the simplest (although not the easiest) to apply. If what you're doing isn't working, stop doing it. Do nothing; do something—almost anything—different. But don't continue down the road you started on, because it will take you somewhere that you don't want to go. This is not as easy as it sounds. In fact, the more time you have spent preparing (and preparing is a good thing), the harder it might be for you to drop it and deal with the situation as it actually is. That is the paradox of planning, and why it is good to consider "what-ifs" when you plan.

Once you have stopped yourself, there are two ways to go. Here is where it is really helpful to know yourself as an influencer. If you are the kind of person who does best with some time to think before you act, go straight to the most important indirect influence technique (see Chapter 18) and disengage. Be open about it, you'll get some credit for paying attention. And you'll keep your foot out of your mouth. Say, "That's interesting. I'd like to think about what you just told me. Let's get together again tomorrow" (or next week, this afternoon, even after a short break if time is pressing). Then think about your plan in the context of the new information and adjust it.

If you are the sort of influencer who thinks out loud, who does best by staying in the situation and working with it, go immediately to receptive behavior if you are not already there. Use the inquire and listen behaviors and keep doing it until you have as much new information as you need. Then you can decide whether or not you want to disengage in order to confer with others or to redesign your approach.

Dealing with Defensiveness, Resistance, and Avoidance

You were only being reasonable, so why on earth did he get so defensive? Or why can't you schedule a meeting with your colleague to discuss this issue? Why is she always "too busy"? Why does your spouse have a last-minute reason not to go to every single meeting you have scheduled with the new contractor?

You will often be puzzled by the nature of someone's response to your attempts to influence him or her. He or she may not behave in the way that you planned or assumed that he or she would. And it is hard to treat this behavior as a valuable source of information (rather than a secret plot to make you crazy), but it is.

First, assume that the person is not actually bad, wrong, or stupid, but in fact, that he or she is behaving in a way that makes perfect sense, given the way the person understands the situation. In order to find out how he or she understands it, so you can correct or deal with it, you can try to "reverse engineer" from the response to the interpretation. You can do that in two ways. Sometimes you can simply ask, in a neutral and curious way: "I've noticed that you haven't been able to make any of the meetings with the contractor. I wonder if there is a reason why you'd just as soon not see him right now?" If you do this, it is absolutely essential that the other person read the subtext (unstated but important meaning) as saying, "You are a reasonable person and I know you are behaving in a rational way. Help me understand it." Any hint of sarcasm or talking down to the other will be fatal to achieving your goal.

If direct influence is not available to you (the other person has left the room in a huff, slammed down the telephone, called you bad names, or simply hasn't been heard from for weeks), then you have another option. Think your way into his or her skin for a moment and ask yourself, "I am reacting as if I have something to lose or something to fear; what is it?" Because defensive, resistant, and avoidance behavior is a normal, fight-or-flight mammalian self-protective response, the answer to that question is often quite clear. You may be surprised or hurt that the other person would think you were capable of something like that, but you will have to get over it if you want to influence. Don't make the person's misjudgment of you the issue. Instead, consider it an interesting, if incorrect, assumption and work with it, using curiosity rather than self-protection.

Once you have an idea of what is going on for the other person, you have a new influence opportunity: you will need to convince her or him that you are not intending to do the thing that he or she fears. (Or if you are, you need to forget about influencing that person yourself. You cannot influence others to appreciate and welcome what they see as threatening when you are the source of that threat.)

Managing Yourself

As much as I may see influence as an opportunity to affect the course of someone else's behavior, the only behavior I can affect directly is my own. The success or failure of an influence opportunity is determined, largely, by how well I can do that.

As part of your preparation, you have examined your own wants, needs, attitudes, and assumptions related to this opportunity. In the actual situation, you will put that information to work. For example, you will notice when your own issues are getting in the way of moving toward your goal.

The following signs indicate that you need to manage your own behavior:

- You or the other person are experiencing a "fight-or-flight" reaction. Some signs of an excess of adrenaline in the system are external, such as an outburst of angry words or a threat to leave the room or the meeting; some are internal, physical stress responses such as a tight throat or gastrointestinal upset.

- The other person has not said anything for some time.

- You are moving further away from your goal as the conversation proceeds.

- The other person is becoming more resistant or defensive.

- You are acting as if your goal was to make the other person wrong.

Sometimes the best way to manage yourself and the situation is to disengage temporarily (see Chapter 18) and reflect on what is going on; you may be able to return with a more productive approach. In any case, you will be more in charge of yourself. You can sometimes ask the other person to take a time-out with you, discuss the way the meeting or conversation is going, and think of a better way to proceed. This must be done in an objective way. Blaming the other person for the problems you are having in influencing him or her will only escalate those problems. Even in very difficult situations, asking for feedback and/or disclosing can turn the situation around. For example, I have found that if I notice that I am becoming excessively self-righteous or defensive and call myself on it before the other person does, this action invariably brings a measure of good humor to the conversation. This can clear the way for influence to occur.

One of the most effective and most difficult self-management tasks is that of consciously making the other person look more intelligent, more reasonable, more well-intentioned than you believe him or her to be. It is one exaggeration that will work to your benefit as an influencer. People tend to live up—or down—to your expectations of them. In summary, managing yourself is perhaps the most difficult aspect of being an effective influencer. It requires an ability to acknowledge your own ego needs and tendencies toward self-deception and to treat them with gentleness and a certain affectionate humor, without being limited by them. In other words, you have to be a grownup about influence in order to keep your inner child from throwing a tantrum at the wrong time or hiding in the closet for fear of punishment.

The Uses of Silence

One of the most underused and effective influence techniques is that of keeping your mouth shut. We humans have a habit of getting in our own way by stepping on the other person's lines or interrupting his or her thought process. We are sometimes so afraid of silence that we answer our own questions and argue both sides of an issue, thereby doing the other person's work (and not, it goes without saying, influencing anyone but ourselves).

The most important ideas we express, the most important questions that we ask, need to be followed by enough silence to allow the other person time to consider (especially if he or she is a classic introvert and likes to think before responding). In fact, this silence can be where influence occurs, because in the end, influence happens in the other person.

Mostly, we don't let the silence happen because we are afraid of being interrupted. We are concerned that we will forget where we were going, that the other will take the lead in the conversation. Remember under those circumstances that, if you have done your planning, you will be confident enough to find your way back to leading or guiding the conversation, once again, toward your goal. And, because influence is always a dialogue, you may learn something in the process.

Making It Up on the Fly

In our fast-paced lives, opportunities for influence come and go in a flash. You won't always have time to plan. Still, there are a few things that you can keep in mind to help you when you have to take influence action on the fly.

- Think of what your goal is for the interaction and then keep it in front of you. If it seems to be retreating into the distance, change course.

- Maintain a balance between expressive and receptive behavior. If you are not making progress, switch to the other kind.

- Never say or do anything that makes the other look or feel bad, wrong, or stupid, especially if there are other people around.

- Treat resistance as a source of information.

- Be curious rather than defensive.

And remember, if what you are doing isn't working, stop doing it. Nothing works all the time, even with the same person or in the same situation. In day-to-day influence, the best approach is akin to the scientific method. Know what you want to achieve, make an educated guess about how best to achieve it, experiment actively, be objective about the outcome, and be ready to try again until you succeed or realize that you are not going to accomplish the result you hope for.

In Part III, we'll examine some special issues in influence: the ethical implications of being an active influencer, the use of electronic media to influence, the means for influencing indirectly, and some ideas for next steps in your growth as an active influencer.

PART II

Planning for Influence

CHAPTER 16

The Ethics of Influence

*"The moral sense is always supported by the permanent interest
of the parties. Else, I know not how, in our world, any good could
ever get done."*

—Ralph Waldo Emerson

Manipulation Versus Influence

In our Exercising Influence workshops, the issue of manipulation
often arises. Many people are concerned about the ethical implications of being conscious and tactical about influence. There is some
confusion about the distinction between manipulation and influence.
A thesaurus suggests the following distinction: to *manipulate* is to
maneuver, handle, exploit, or deceive. To *influence* is to induce,
incite, persuade, or activate. Influence implies respect for the other;
manipulation does not. There is nothing fundamentally unethical or
dishonest about choosing your behavior and words deliberately in
order to persuade or activate others to join you in taking action.

When asked the question, "How do you know that you have
been manipulated?" groups of managers and leaders consistently say,
"When the other has been dishonest with me, leading me to take an
action I would not have taken otherwise." When asked, "How do

you know that you have been influenced?" the typical reply is, "I voluntarily choose to change or take action based on what the other did or said."

Thus, there are two key issues that distinguish one from the other: (1) trust in the honesty of the influencer and (2) a sense of choice about the action. Influence implies individual choice based on trustworthy information and guidance.

Several factors may cause people to be manipulative. Sometimes it is simply a skill or experience deficit; we are doing what has been done to us. Sometimes we wish to avoid the appearance of using direct power and hope that people will believe they are making a real choice. Sometimes we are fearful of the conflict that may result from telling the truth, so we maintain a hidden agenda and hope things go our way without having to reveal it. Sometimes we have simply not done our homework and are choosing an expedient way to involve another person. And there are certain pathological personality disorders that lead some people to be consistently manipulative.

Expressive influence becomes manipulative when we:

- Make up or distort facts to support our positions

- Imply that we share goals that we do not, in fact, share

- Promise things that we know we cannot deliver

- Make threats we don't have the power or will to carry out

- Imply that powerful others will take actions (the equivalent of "wait until your father comes home") without having checked this out in advance

- Fail to warn the other of important consequences of taking or not taking an action

- Express a vision that we know to be unrealistic or impossible to achieve or that we do not really believe in

- Flatter the other insincerely to encourage him or her to join or support us

Receptive influence becomes manipulative when we:

- Ask for information, then use it to harm or embarrass the other

- Twist the other's words, intentions, or motivations in the guise of listening and attempting to understand

- Show false empathy when we in fact are judgmental

- Invite the other to be open and vulnerable without reciprocating

- Imply in any subtle way that the other is bad, wrong, or stupid to believe as he or she does

- Reject any ideas or suggestions the other comes up with in response, unless and until we hear the "right answer"

- Invite the other to take action as if it were his or her responsibility and then use power, sarcasm, or ridicule to attempt to stop him or her from taking the action

The ethical influencer must ask him- or herself the following questions:

- Am I telling the literal truth, as far as I know, where any objective data is involved? Have I left out any key information that the other should know before making a choice?

- Am I being honest about my own opinions, beliefs, intentions, enthusiasm, and commitment when I have expressed them? Have I been open about my intention to influence the other?

- Am I willing and do I have the option to take "no" for an answer?

- Am I willing and do I have the option to allow the other to take a different action from the one I would prefer?

- Is this an issue that can best be dealt with through influence rather than the use of direct power that I have or can borrow? If not, am I willing to use that power openly?

Influence and Self-Interest

One of the great ethical responsibilities of the influencer is to be aware of his or her motivation in relation to the influence goal. It is perfectly legitimate to serve your own interests as long as you are not working against the interests of those you choose to influence or of the institutions or systems of which you are both members and to whom you owe respect and loyalty. Thus, influencing someone to disobey a legitimate rule or law (one you were both aware of and, in essence, signed up to uphold) can be unethical, whereas influencing someone to work with you to change a rule or law you believe to be unfair would be ethical. Influencing someone to help you do something that would benefit you but could be harmful to him or her would be unethical, unless you were completely honest about the risks involved and the person had free choice.

It is also important not to misuse your knowledge of others' self-interest or vulnerability to guide them in a direction you know would have serious negative consequences for them or others.

What Doesn't Work

I think the behaviors that I'm going to name below are not only ineffective, but also unethical, although often done with the best of intentions. These actions are based on the unexamined assumption that other people are mean, foolish, fearful, or unimportant and don't deserve to be treated with respect. They include:

- Threatening

- Whining

- Tit-for-tat

- Ridiculing

- Shaming

- Anything else that attempts to make the other look or feel bad, wrong, or stupid

When these behaviors work, it is only while you are watching, and only if you have sufficient power. None of them actually influences anyone, since influence is something that requires the participation and agreement of the other.

CHAPTER 17

Influencing Electronically

"Words are also actions, and actions are a kind of words."

—Ralph Waldo Emerson

The Wonders and Terrors of Instant Communication

There is nothing that will make the effects of a vacation or long weekend disappear faster than the realization that we have thirty-two voice mails or hundreds of e-mail messages to deal with. The electronic networks that were supposed to make our lives easier and more efficient have become sticky spiderwebs of complexities that attract and trap time and effort.

Because of the mobility of many families, electronic media have become more and more important in communicating with one another. With children who are away at college, spouses and partners who are doing business in another part of the world, parents who have retired and moved, and siblings and friends who live far away, our personal lives are also filled with opportunities to influence electronically.

Like it or not, we live in a world in which we must communicate with and influence people whom we seldom see. Realistically, much of our communication, and thus much of our influencing, will take place through these channels. We might as well learn to do it in the most effective way we can.

Electronic influence has advantages and disadvantages related to the immediacy of the medium. This can be positive when it is important to find support or make team decisions quickly. Both voice mail and e-mail differ from real-time, instant communication (such as a face-to-face discussion) in that there is a record left that can be shared with others for whom the message was not intended.

Influencing electronically is challenging and should probably not be your first choice for important opportunities if other means are at hand. In some organizations, people who sit in adjacent offices or cubicles will send e-mails in preference to speaking directly, especially about difficult issues. Unfortunately, the perceived importance, and thus the impact of a message, is often directly related to the effort and risk the sender has put forth.

Some situations in which e-mail, or even voice mail, is not a good means of communicating or influencing include:

- When the issue is complex or urgent and the other person is potentially accessible

- When there is a conflict involved and the other person may see you as attempting to avoid it

- When you want the other person to understand how important the issue is to you

- When you want the other person to recognize how important his or her opinion is to you

- When you need time to draw the other person out in order to gain his or her ideas and support

In all of these cases and others, it is best if you can arrange a face-to-face meeting or, if that is not possible, a telephone meeting or a video or computer real-time conference.

A common problem with e-mail, in particular, is that people tend to treat it as if it were a conversation and do not plan or screen their remarks. Once a message has been sent, it is difficult to unsend it. And you don't know how many other people have had an opportunity to eavesdrop on the conversation.

E-mail and voice mail in general follow the same principles of influence as do face-to-face influence opportunities. The behaviors are the same, although you don't have the reinforcement of voice tone (with e-mail), facial expressions, or gestures to clarify the meaning of your words. Over time, you should balance expressive and receptive influence; you can often include both types of behavior in the same message. In fact, it is often a good idea to err on the side of receptive behavior, since you have fewer clues as to how the other person is reacting than you do in face-to-face interactions.

Learning how to use these media in conscious and productive ways can greatly expand your sphere of influence. While many people today communicate continually through electronic means, few have developed the skills to use these influence opportunities well. Failing to do so can lead not only to missed opportunities, but also to unprecedented and costly misunderstandings and conflicts.

First, You Have to Get Their Attention . . .

Influence messages require a response so that you know whether you are getting closer to or further from your goal. Among the large number of communications most business people receive daily, only a few will earn a thoughtful response. Given limitations of time and energy, we tend to select the ones that look most important or interesting.

These will probably include:

- Messages from people who are key to our success or with whom we have an important relationship

- Messages about something in which we have an immediate interest or strong need

- Messages that look as if we will not get into trouble by the way we respond

- Messages that can be responded to easily and quickly

- Messages that are sent to us personally, rather than to a long list

- Messages that are brief and succinct; large blocks of text are not likely to invite the recipient to review the message quickly

We are unlikely to respond quickly or productively to messages when we perceive that our responses will create problems or more work for us, provide no benefits, or have no impact on anything we care about.

Knowing this, it is possible to design messages so they are more likely to attract the recipient's attention. First, the recipient must be interested enough to open the message rather than ignore it. Next, he or she must read and respond to it. The subject line of your message should influence the recipient to open and read it, if your name alone won't do it (and it probably won't unless you are the person's boss, best friend, or current romantic interest). A subject line that reads, "I need your inspirations about a topic for the meeting," for example, will probably get a better hearing than, "Why haven't I heard from you?" Electronic whining is still whining.

Let the other person know up-front, in the first line or two, what you need and why he or she would benefit from responding to your message. For example, "Tell me where you think we should hold our next meeting. I want to make sure you don't have to travel as far as you did last month. I need to book the meeting by Friday." In this case, the response needed is clear, the benefits are obvious, and the deadline is specific. If it is necessary to send a long message electronically, breaking the message into shorter segments through the use of bullets or numbered lists can help.

Anything you can do to make it easy to respond by phone or return e-mail, such as offering options A, B, or C, will make it easier and thus more likely that you will receive a response. When you leave a message on voice mail, it may be helpful to brief (and it should be very brief!) the person on the issue, then say that there is no need to call back unless a discussion is needed. Say that, otherwise, you will assume the other person accepts or supports the idea or will attend the meeting or commit to the responsibility. This works best with relatively simple and non-controversial messages; it can save time and is useful in uncovering areas of disagreement of which you were not aware.

Stimulating a Productive Response

As in any other form of influencing, creating defensiveness is to be avoided at all costs. Using words that are accusatory or inflammatory will create a fight-or-flight reaction, just as it would in real time. Either you will not hear back from the person, or you will hear something you would rather not have heard. In either case, no influence will occur.

Use words that are nonjudgmental, businesslike, and that assume that the other will respond productively. It also helps to acknowledge your understanding that it will require some time and effort on the other's part, but avoid obsequiousness.

A good example: "I know you are on a tight deadline. Let me know a good time to get ten minutes with you to review the report."

A bad example: "I suppose you'll be too busy to meet with me again."

Preventing Misunderstandings, Embarrassment, and Other E-Mail Disasters

All of us have heard stories of e-mail disasters, such as the man who sent his girlfriend a very explicit love letter and accidentally copied it to everyone in the company. Most e-mail disasters, however, occur because we "write out loud" and then press the "send" button without thinking about how the other might react, or whether this message will help achieve an influence goal.

The one certain way to prevent such occurrences is to leave some time between composing an important e-mail message—one that is intended to influence—and sending it. This is almost an unnatural act, given the instantaneous nature of most e-mail communication, but it has many benefits.

A good exercise is to write the message as a first draft, then set it aside for a while. (Even a few minutes can help.) Reread it and ask yourself the following questions:

- What is my influence goal here?

- Am I using the most effective possible behaviors to achieve that goal? What might work better?

- Is there a balance between expressive and receptive influence?

- What other interpretations of my words might be possible? Is there any possibility the other person might be put off or made defensive by any of these interpretations? What is the "worst case" interpretation he or she might make?

Err on the pessimistic side of things; it is amazing what people can read into messages if they are having a particularly paranoid sort of day. Once you have identified all possible misunderstandings (or, for that matter, correct understandings that won't help you reach your goal—yes, you really do think the marketing VP is a yo-yo, but you have to do business with him!), you will want to rewrite the message. Send a really important influence message only when you have reviewed it at least twice (and sometimes it is good to have someone else whom you trust look at it as well).

Text and Instant Messaging and Beyond

Many forms of messaging are becoming more ubiquitous and insistent. Text messaging is not an especially useful influence medium, as it tends to be used primarily for brief and simple communications— at least as of this writing and while it is dependent on thumb dexterity. It can be useful, however, to point the recipient toward an important message that you send in another way. (Pls chk e-mail 2 u.) Instant messaging, however, creates the opportunity for a conversation in real time and can certainly be used to influence others.

Taking time to review your response before sending, as you would with e-mail, only faster, is the key to effective IM influence.

As Internet telephony becomes more ubiquitous and as we stay connected to our mobile phones and communications devices continually, we will be living in a world where influence can happen with anyone, anywhere, at any time. (For the introverts among us, this may not be good news.)

CHAPTER 18

Influencing Indirectly

"The best effect of fine persons is felt after we have left their presence."
—Ralph Waldo Emerson

What Is Indirect Influence?

Indirect influence means simply that you keep your influence goal in mind and take some action other than dealing directly with the person or group whom you wish to influence. This can mean either that you work through other people or that you use other means to accomplish your goal. Indirect influence is normally done in the open, however, and should not be confused with manipulation, in which your motivations and agenda are intentionally hidden.

When Is Indirect Influence Appropriate?

Most of the time it will be easier to influence others directly. Here are some situations in which that may not be as effective:

- You do not have access to the target person or group because of political, geographic, language, cultural, or other considerations.

- You do not currently have a good influence relationship with the other person and the issue is urgent enough that you don't have the time to build one.

- You are not perceived by the other to have the relevant knowledge, expertise, or status that would be the appropriate power sources for this influence issue.

- The issue is a major one and you simply don't have the power to be effective directly.

- You have been using direct methods and have hit a snag or are at an impasse.

These situations and others like them will lead you to consider other means of influencing.

Influencing Through Other Individuals

Sometimes the best solution is to find someone who is in a better position to influence the target person than you are and delegate the influencing to him or her. (Of course, this will require you to influence that person to take on the responsibility of influencing the target person or group.)

If this is your best option, be sure to discuss your influence goal very thoroughly with the other person and give him or her the benefit of the planning work you have done. You are giving up some control of the specific outcome in exchange for the chance to achieve your goal, so it is essential that you trust the other person and share all relevant information, including your own areas of flexibility. You should also be very open to this person's advice regarding your goal; he or she will have to believe in it to be able to achieve it for you or your team.

Influencing as Part of a Group

When an issue is extremely important or affects a great many people, or when the influence target is at some political or hierarchical distance, you will want to consider organizing a group in order to influence. One middle manager's opinion may not count for much with the COO, but a cross-functional committee of concerned managers may be able to get a hearing. One son or daughter may not be able to convince an elderly parent to give up the privilege of driving, but all the siblings acting in concert may be effective.

It often takes not only a large number, but also a broad coalition of people and vested interests to influence senior corporate or government officials to take action or change course. It is easy to dismiss a small homogeneous group as "a bunch of cranks," but much more difficult to do so when they represent diverse aspects of the community. On the other hand, recent research suggests that change can happen rapidly when the right people with a powerful idea "tip the balance."[7]

Debate as an Indirect Influence Tactic

One common approach that does not work well as a direct influence tactic, although it has other important uses, is debating. This often comes as a surprise to people, especially those who are more analytical. While debating an issue can develop strong ideas and make sure that bad ideas don't go unchallenged, it is a contest of ideas and positions with winners and losers. The greatest influence impact is on those who are listening to and/or judging the debate. Since most debate is focused on proving that your position is right and the other's position is wrong, the debaters are likely to become more firmly fixed in the rightness of their cause or opinion, rather than influencing one another. Thus, you can debate with another person as a way of influencing a third party (of course, it's best if both debaters are aware that this is what they are doing), but there is little hope of influencing the other debater.

Disengaging as a Means to an End

Disengaging can be an effective way to manage time, authority issues, and relationships. Sometimes moving away temporarily can help you to reach a satisfactory outcome when moving forward would only create greater resistance or loss of an opportunity.

Sometimes it is useful to maintain your individual connection to the influence target, but move to a different set of tactics. For example, when you are at an impasse (or, preferably, when you see that you are headed in that direction but before it occurs), you can choose to disengage temporarily. My husband, who is particularly good at this tactic, used to say in a line reminiscent of a popular commercial for wine, "Let's make no decision before its time; we can discuss this later." Artfully, he always manages to do this just before I have committed to an absolute "no" on the issue. This tactic allows the use of persistence and timing to have its effect. When you choose to disengage, it's important to let the other know that you'll be back—and often to establish when you will reconvene. This prevents disengagement from looking like retreat.

Of course, there will be times when you recognize that there is no point in continuing an influence attempt, given the time and energy it looks as if it will take compared to the likelihood and value of success. In that case, disengagement may be permanent. (It may also provide an opportunity to refocus your influence plan on a more appropriate goal or a different person.) You can still gain some influence value from such a situation by being graceful rather than huffy about it. "I can see that this issue is of great importance to you. As long as you are willing to take the major responsibility for seeing that it gets done, I'm willing to do it your way." Then let go of the issue completely, rather than wait in hiding until something goes wrong so you can say, "I told you so." You'll pay for that. This is an example of "disarming" or letting go of issues that are more important to the other than to you and saving your influence energy for issues that you care about more. This may create a sense of fairness and reasonableness that you can call on later. On the other hand, you may be better off using such opportunities for more direct negotiation. A quid pro quo that is a done deal is more effective than "you owe me one"—something that is almost never remembered in the same way by both parties.

Using Other Means to Influence Indirectly

When you do not have access to a "subject-matter expert" and the issue involves knowledge that the other person does not think you have, influencing through books and articles by people that he or she respects may be helpful. This is better done early in the process, however, rather than as an "I told you so" attempt that is likely to inspire a defensive and resistant response.

Finally, one of the most useful indirect influence tools (a form of disengaging briefly) is the use of humor. Knowing when to use a story, joke, or wry comment to relieve tension or keep the encounter from going too far in the wrong direction is an art. But there is one clear rule about the use of humor in influencing. It should NEVER be used in a sarcastic manner or in any way that might reflect negatively on the other person or something he or she holds dear. It should be either slightly self-deprecating or directed at a force or third party that you both consider a "common enemy." And you must also be artful about bringing the conversation back toward where you want it to go.

CHAPTER 19

Applied Influence

Making Things Happen

"This time, like all times, is a very good one, if we but know what to do with it."

—Ralph Waldo Emerson

Maintaining and Improving Your Influence Fitness

You have developed your influence skills, mapped the territory, prepared, and implemented your plan for a specific influence situation. By now, you probably know whether this is a set of skills you really want to develop. As in any fitness program, your progress will depend on your willingness to be conscious, focused, and disciplined about regular practice. Ideally, as in a gym or fitness center, you will start with some simple, low-impact exercises and move on to ones that are more complex and risky as you become more skillful. If you want to become more powerful, graceful, and flexible as an influencer, there is no better exercise than to decide on a goal and consciously go after it. Following are some ideas to think about and some experiments to try at work, at home, and in your community.

Making Things Happen at Work

A component of making things happen at work is the recognition that comes with being seen as an effective influencer. In today's flatter, more team-based organizations, leadership through influence is highly respected and valued. It is reasonable to expect that effective influence behavior will be related to career success. But, because it requires a willingness to risk, to be open about, and to stand up for your ideas and opinions, it also exposes you to jealousy and competitiveness. You will fail more often because you are initiating action more often. You will find it difficult to become less visible, even if you want to be.

A *Fortune* magazine article[8] suggested that the one thing that unsuccessful CEOs had in common was a "failure to execute." (I did think that was rather obvious until I thought of a few failed CEOs who had executed the wrong thing only too well.) I would revise that to suggest that executives and other leaders fail most when they have a good idea and are unable to influence others to own it and make it happen.

Try This at Work

Here are some suggestions about using your influence skills at work. Try one or two of them every day in a conscious way, and take a minute afterward to reflect on how the interaction went and what you learned from doing it. If you choose to influence someone with whom you are in a high-trust relationship, ask for feedback. Acknowledge that you are working on being more effective as an influencer. Ask what he or she noticed about your approach and how you could be more effective.

- Influence a co-worker to reschedule a meeting that is inconvenient for you.

- Influence a team member to take on another responsibility.

- Influence your manager to send you to an important professional conference.

- Influence your client to extend a deadline for deliverables.

- Influence your manager to implement a change in the way projects are assigned.

- Influence a decision-maker to use a vendor that you prefer.

- Influence a colleague to substitute for you at a meeting.

- Influence your manager to provide more resources for your project.

- Influence a direct report to take on additional responsibilities.

- Influence a peer to support your controversial proposal.

- Influence a colleague to help you meet a deadline on an important project.

- Influence a senior manager in another part of the organization to sponsor an innovative idea.

The next time a colleague or manager turns down your request, try using receptive behavior (inquire or facilitate) to learn what is in the way or what it would take for him or her to say "yes" to you; then use negotiate behavior to firm up an agreement.

Making Things Happen at Home

By contrast, you will usually want to make things happen at home through influence without being recognized as the "mover and shaker." You will probably go out of your way to balance the influence relationships in your family or household (this is not the same as balancing the power relationships, which is not appropriate in families with young children). You have an opportunity to model a way of accomplishing results that helps everyone in the household feel both involved and committed and to develop a set of skills that will pay lifelong dividends. If there are children in the household, you will be offering them the invaluable gift of learning how to make things happen in their own lives in a way that is respectful of others, empowering to themselves and the family, and productive of results.

It is a good idea to let people who are close to you know up-front that you are going to be trying some new approaches and to enlist them in supporting you. Even though a partner, spouse, or friend might have been telling you that you should change, when you do it requires something different in the way of a response from them. Humans are paradoxical creatures, and sometimes we prefer behavior that is "the devil we know" to something that is unfamiliar, even though we have asked for the change. This can sometimes lead to a lack of support for positive change on your part that you will find surprising and painful. If you keep important others "in the loop" from the beginning, they will have time to get used to the idea, feel included in the process, and be more likely to offer the encouragement and feedback that you need.

Try This at Home

There are many opportunities daily to influence the people you live with or to whom you are close. Here are a few ideas to start with:

- Influence a family member to take on a new household responsibility.

- Influence your spouse or partner to try a new restaurant or see a movie that would normally not appeal to him or her.

- Influence a child to complete his or her homework an hour earlier than usual.

- Influence a spouse, partner, or friend to take responsibility for weekend plans.

- Influence an older child to keep you better informed about his or her whereabouts.

- Influence a spouse, partner, or friend to take a vacation to a destination that is new to both of you.

- Influence a friend or family member to cook a meal for you.

- Influence a partner, friend, or spouse to invest with you in a business opportunity.

- Influence a young family member or friend to apply to a specific college or academic program that you believe would be a good fit.

- Influence a spouse or partner to purchase a home or vacation property.

- Influence a young person to tell you about a dream he or she has for the future or a problem he or she is experiencing.

- Influence an elderly parent to stop driving.

- Influence a household member to fix the broken "whatsiz" that you have all been putting up with for several months.

The next time you and a spouse, partner, or other family member start into a familiar conflict that usually ends in an impasse, interrupt the process by using receptive behavior (inquire, listen, or attune) to understand his or her needs, concerns, issues, or point of view.

Making Things Happen in Your Community

Making things happen in your community means that you will be asked to do so again and again. Fortunately, if you are an effective influencer, you will not have to do it alone. You will have the support of people who are willing to put effort into things that you and they care about. Very few things that we care about in our communities can be accomplished alone. By using your influence skills, you will help create a network of people who will continue the important work.

Try This in Your Community

Here are some possible influence opportunities in your community. You will think of many more.

- Influence an important person to speak to your organization or serve on your committee.

- Influence a department of your local government or association to give you permission to build a nonconforming addition to your house.

- Influence a friend or neighbor to join you in promoting or sponsoring a community event.

- Influence your child's teacher to allow him or her to accompany you on a vacation trip outside of school holidays.

- Influence a group of neighbors to join together in obtaining permission for and creating a community garden on an empty lot in your neighborhood.

- Influence a clergy member in your church or synagogue to preach a sermon on a topic of interest to you.

- Influence your local government or association to change or modify a regulation that is inconvenient or unnecessary.

- Influence your neighbor to attend a meeting on a topic of interest to you.

- Influence others in your community to donate to a cause that you believe to be important.

The next time you are disappointed in the kind of service or response you are receiving from an organization or official in your community, use expressive influence to voice your concerns and all the influence skills at your disposal to gain others' support in changing the situation.

Influence skills, like all skills, are developed through practice, feedback, and re-practice. By finding opportunities to influence and consciously choosing and using these skills every day, your "influence muscles" will continue to grow stronger. Just as you need to cool down after exercising in the gym, you can cool down after exercising influence by reflecting on the experience. Think about what worked and what did not and decide how to take that learning forward to the next opportunity.

Afterword

The Paradox of Failure

"Every moment instructs, and every object: for wisdom is infused into every form."

—Ralph Waldo Emerson

SO . . . YOU SET YOUR GOAL, did your homework, got the support you needed, planned, and executed. And you failed. You didn't influence the other person after all that. Your daughter still went off to Europe alone. The boss wouldn't approve your project. The recalcitrant committee members gave a minority report. How do you deal with it?

First, sit down and have a nice cup of tea. Call a friend. Rant and rave. Or, if you prefer, read a trashy novel or watch an old movie with a lot of car crashes in it. Get used to it, though, because once you start being conscious about influencing, you will notice that you fail a lot. Of course, this is because you are paying attention rather than doing the blindfolded drive-by influencing you used to prefer. You are failing because you are taking risks—and it is the nature of risk to be associated with failure as much as with success.

But after you get past the first twenty minutes or so of teeth-gnashing, you will acknowledge that you have, after all, had partial successes, and here and there a really glorious moment. And you will probably notice also that you have learned a lot from the things that didn't work and that you feel more in charge of your own life than you used to. Being the persistent person you are, you will continue to try to shape the events that make your world. You will develop a better sense of humor. And you will live to influence another day. Here is one last favorite Emerson quote:

"All promise outruns the performance. We live in a system of approximations. Every end is prospective of some other end, which is also temporary; a round and final success nowhere. We are encamped in nature, not domesticated."

What? So What? Now What?

That about sums up the way to treat your influence experiences. If what you are doing isn't working, you can stop doing it. You would probably rather not reproduce the same mistakes (to quote George Santayana, "Those who cannot learn from the past will be condemned to repeat it"). You will probably want to remember what worked well so you can do it again. It's worth your while to take some time to reflect about an influence opportunity just after it is over. A quick formula for this is to use: What? So what? Now what? What happened, what does it mean, and what am I going to do about it?

Then pick up that novel and go to the beach.

APPENDIX A

Coaching Partnerships

THE IDEAL COACHING PARTNER for learning influence skills is a person who is different from you in some important ways. Some of those differences could include:

- Skills and abilities

- Role

- Profession

- Goals and vested interests

The differences are important because they will enable you to provide objective feedback to one another and to have a richer set of experiences and skills to draw from. At the same time, you need to have a set of shared values and a shared commitment to learning and improving. A high degree of mutual trust is a prerequisite to working together in this way.

You and your coaching partner will begin with an initial session to establish goals and a plan for subsequent sessions. Ideally, each of you will have completed the first section of the book. In addition, you may wish to use the *Exercising Influence Workbook: A Self-Study Guide* (see Note 5). During the first meeting, which may take an hour or so, you should try to do most of the following activities. Make sure you leave time for both of you to complete each activity.

1. Do the "Sphere of Influence" exercise together and discuss it.

2. Identify typical influence situations that occur in your lives.

3. Share some longer-term goals you would like to achieve that will require improved influencing skills.

4. Decide on one or two areas in which you would like to focus your practice at first. These should be actions that you believe you should do more often or more effectively to help you to achieve your goals.

5. Select an upcoming influence opportunity that you can prepare for in the next session.

6. Set a time for your next session.

In subsequent meetings, you may want to do some of the following activities:

1. Prepare for an upcoming influence opportunity by using the Influence Plan in Appendix B and consulting with your partner.

   • Set a goal.

   • Develop the influence framework.

   • Choose the most useful behaviors.

   • Practice the scenario with your partner.

   • Stop and start the scenario to obtain feedback from your partner as to whether you are moving closer to your goal. Ask for suggestions as to what might work better.

   • Try it in several different ways by asking your partner to respond differently and/or by trying different behaviors.

2. Choose a specific behavior to practice and have your partner "feed" you situations that you want to use for practice. For example, suppose you want to practice listen behavior. Your partner might launch the following scenarios:

   - Your manager has just told you that you cannot go to a seminar you had been planning on attending.

   - Your colleague has canceled a standing meeting for the third time without explanation.

   - Your teenage son or daughter has informed you that a friend has offered hang-gliding lessons.

3. Your partner will respond as if he or she were the person you are influencing. Whatever he or she says, you will respond by using listen behaviors. Stop after a few minutes and ask your partner what was going on. Did he or she become more or less open to influence through the process? What worked well about the way you responded? What could be improved? Try the same situations with a different behavior. Focus more on practicing the behavior than on achieving the goal.

4. Identify opportunities to practice a specific skill in the real world before your next meeting, and commit to debriefing your experiences with your partner.

APPENDIX B

Influence Plan

Part 1

Following are a series of questions that fall within each of the areas of the influence framework. Review the questions in each area and highlight the ones that you believe to be relevant to the outcome of your influence opportunity. Answer the key questions, then think how you will use the information to build the relationship, and achieve your desired results.

Results

- What is your vision of success? What role will the other person play in it?

- What are the needs that underlie your vision? For you? For the organization? For the person you are influencing?

- What specific long-term and short-term goals do you have for the influence opportunity?

- What are your criteria for success? How will you know you have achieved the results you are aiming for?

- What alternative outcomes might satisfy the underlying needs and achieve equivalent results?

Exercising Influence, Revised Edition. Copyright © 2007 by John Wiley & Sons, Inc.
Reproduced by permission of Pfeiffer, an Imprint of Wiley. www.pfeiffer.com

Relationship

- What is the history of your (or your team's) influence relationship (in both directions) with this person or group?

- What is the current level of trust? Why?

- What assumptions do each of you hold about the other? How will you test them? How might they affect the outcome?

- What is the power balance between you?

- What are the current or continuing issues in the relationship, regardless of whether they are directly related to this influence opportunity?

Context

- Individual

  What are the relevant values of the other? How are they similar or different from yours?

  What are his or her high-priority goals right now? Yours?

  What common or conflicting vested interests are important in this situation? What do each of you have to gain or lose?

  What are the important current issues that have an impact on this person?

  How would you describe his or her communication or work style? How does he or she generally prefer to be approached? How does your usual approach match with his or her preferences? How might you want to modify it?

- Organizational

  How does the business strategy of the organization relate to the subject at hand? Are the results you envision a good "fit" for the organizational strategy and goals?

How will the organization's structure and processes affect your influence approach? Is your approach out of the norm?

Where does this issue stand in the ranking of organizational priorities?

How might the formal or informal power structure in the organization affect the outcome of your influence action?

Who are other stakeholders in the outcome of your action? How will you involve them?

- Cultural

What are the cultural values (organizational, professional, national, or ethnic) that are relevant to this issue?

What are the norms (formal or informal ground rules) that you should be aware of?

What are some of the cultural assumptions that relate to this situation?

What are the usual cultural practices or rituals that might be useful in this situation?

Are there any cultural taboos that could derail your approach?

Behavior

- Given your analysis of the situation, what do you intend your influence behaviors to achieve?

- What are the best specific behaviors to achieve those results?

External Trends and Issues

- What is going on right now in the larger systems of which you are a part that could have an impact on your influence opportunity?

Part 2

1. Highlight the key questions that you want to explore.

2. Summarize the results.

3. Focus and refine your influence goal.

4. Choose the most applicable behaviors.

5. Plan a sequence.

6. Troubleshoot.

7. Focus on your next steps.

8. Evaluate and learn.

APPENDIX C

Meeting Processes That Support Effective Influencing

SINCE SO MUCH INFLUENCING takes place at formal or informal meetings, whether at work, at home, or in your community, following are some suggestions for designing meetings for effective two-way influencing. If the outcome of the meeting is to be a decision or set of actions that will require the commitment of participants, it is especially important that each person have an opportunity to influence the end result. Too many meetings are designed to avoid engaging people in discussion about decisions that they will have to buy into and implement. This only lengthens the overall process.

1. If you are the person calling the meeting, spend some one-to-one time with other key "stakeholders" (those who have something to gain or lose by the outcome of the meeting) and get their ideas as to what should be on the agenda, who should be invited, and so forth.

2. Send out the agenda or let participants know in advance the topics that will be discussed. That way, those who like to think before they speak out will have a chance to prepare to influence others at the meeting. This tends to shorten the meeting, because people will come prepared. In addition, establishing topics in advance can prevent the situation that

arises when someone who did not participate actively at the last meeting now wants to re-open the topic for discussion, just when you thought the matter was settled.

3. Ask someone to facilitate the meeting. This is especially important if there will be difficult or controversial topics on the agenda, or if the group typically tends to become bogged down in details or get sidetracked. The person who is facilitating should be someone who does not have a vested interest in the outcome of the issues under discussion. This can be a rotating role in your group, or you can use someone outside the group who has had some training in meeting facilitation. The job of the facilitator is to manage the process of the meeting by agreement with other members of the group. He or she should not contribute to the content without stepping out of his or her facilitator role. See the Resources list for suggestions.

4. State clearly in the agenda, and again at the beginning of the meeting, the purpose of the session and the process you will follow. It is helpful for participants to know what results are expected. Which of the following best describes your purpose?

- Communicate information

- Gather information

- Explore problems or issues

- Make a decision

- Announce a decision and discuss how to implement it

- Establish a set of norms or ground rules for this meeting (or to use at all meetings of a particular group) that will ensure that everyone has a fair chance to be heard and to influence the decisions appropriately. Ask participants for suggestions and then be sure to enforce them in a good-natured way. Some examples might be:

Have a time limit for each person's comments on a particular topic

Ask for someone's ideas if he or she has not spoken for a while

Ask the group for alternatives before settling on a solution

5. In meetings that are primarily expressive in nature (such as meetings that communicate information or decisions), it is important to set aside time afterward to use receptive skills to gather questions and/or listen to concerns.

6. In meetings that are primarily receptive in nature (such as meetings that are held for the purpose of gathering information or exploring issues), it is important to begin with an expressive statement informing or reminding participants of the purpose and process and why they are being involved. It may also be useful to share a vision of the ideal results of the meeting and encourage participants to be active and open.

7. Overall, meetings should be designed to enable participants to move back and forth between expressing their ideas and learning about what others think. There is little chance of a successful result if everyone is only interested in expressing his or her ideas—or, for that matter, if no one is willing to take the risk of putting an idea on the table. A good facilitator can be very helpful with this.

8. Use different processes during the meeting to involve everyone who has something to contribute. For example, try a "nominal group process" in which each person contributes a thought or idea, one at a time. (There should always be an option to pass.)

9. Be sure to separate processes that are meant to generate ideas, such as brainstorming, from processes that are evaluative and meant to move toward decision making. Use ground rules

that support the process you are using. (For example, brainstorming processes require a "no evaluation of ideas" ground rule to be successful.)

10. Notice when someone who is key to implementing the group's decision, or whose support is important, is not participating or is giving signals that he or she is not happy with the direction. Use receptive skills to invite that person to participate and/or to express concerns.

11. For important decisions that require participants' support, consider using a consensus process. Consensus does not mean that everyone believes it is the best possible decision. It means that everyone has agreed that he or she can live with, support, and implement the decision. A consensus decision process involves:

    • A proposal for a decision, often a summary of a discussion about the issues involved

    • A question: "Who cannot support the decision as stated?"

    • A query to those who are not in agreement: "What would have to change in order for you to be able to live with and implement the decision?"

    • A discussion and good-faith effort to modify the decision to gain the support of those who disagree

    • Another check for agreement

    This process may be repeated several times until a consensus is reached.

12. Consider who, outside of the group, will need to be influenced in order for any meeting decisions to be implemented successfully. Discuss how to approach the influence "tasks" as next steps in the decision process.

All of the suggestions above are valid, whether the meeting is held face-to-face or by video, telephone, or web conference. When participants in the meeting are not co-located, special care should be taken to make sure that everyone has an opportunity to participate and influence. From time to time, the facilitator or leader in a virtual meeting should do a "round-robin" check for comments, opinions, or questions from each participant by name (always allowing for a "pass" response).

APPENDIX D

Sentence Starters

Expressive Behaviors

Tell

"I recommend that . . ."

"I suggest that we . . ."

"It's important to me that . . ."

"I need . . ."

Sell

"My analysis shows . . ."

"The reasons are . . ."

"This could help us achieve . . ."

"The benefits would be . . ."

Negotiate

"If you will do this, I will . . . "

"In exchange, I'll . . . "

"Here's what I can do to make it work . . . "

"I need to let you know the consequences of . . . "

Enlist

"Here's what I believe could happen . . . "

"I can see us . . . "

"As a team, we can . . . "

"I know you are capable of . . . "

Receptive Behaviors

Inquire

"What do you think about . . . "

"What ideas do you have for . . . "

"Help me understand . . . "

"Tell me more about . . . "

Listen

"So from your point of view . . . "

"Your problem with this is . . . "

"I'm wondering if you're concerned about . . . "

"You seem hesitant. Could that be because. . . ?"

Attune

"I know how busy you are these days . . . "

"If I were in your shoes, I might want . . . "

"You're right. I should have . . . "

"I really need help on . . . "

Facilitate

"So your dilemma is . . . "

"On the one hand . . . and on the other. . . ."

"What would it take for you to . . ."

"How might you go about doing that?"

APPENDIX E

Influence Scenarios

LET'S REVISIT THE SCENARIOS from the beginning of the book. In the following few pages, we'll imagine a better (though not necessarily ideal—that's life!) outcome for each scenario through the conscious use of influence. As you read the scenarios, notice which behavioral skills are being used and how some of the principles discussed in the book are being implemented. These are not intended as "school solutions" to these problems. Rather, they represent one productive way to approach the situation. How might you handle the situations now that you have had a chance to think about the process of influence?

1. It's five o'clock. You have been at your desk since six this morning, and you're nowhere near ready to go home. You have a meeting with your manager tomorrow morning, and you're supposed to have a report finished. You would have, too, if the other people involved had done their parts. First, the data was late from your counterpart in the other group. The people on your team had other priorities and couldn't help you with the analysis. Then the "admin" was too busy to help you print and collate the report. You might have asked your manager for an extension, but you didn't want to look unprepared, so you decided to do it all yourself. It looks like an all-nighter.

Exercising Influence, Revised Edition. Copyright © 2007 by John Wiley & Sons, Inc.
Reproduced by permission of Pfeiffer, an Imprint of Wiley. www.pfeiffer.com

It's two weeks before your report is due. You notice that some of the data you are waiting for is overdue from your counterpart in the other group. You call and arrange to meet him briefly in the cafeteria. Your goal is to obtain a commitment from him to give you the information that you need. Over coffee, you have the following conversation:

- *You:* Kumar, I'm aware that you haven't given the data to me this week, as you had agreed. What's holding it up?

- *Kumar:* Yes, I know. I thought I could, but I have run into a problem.

- *You:* Tell me about the problem.

- *Kumar:* Well, the analyst who started it broke his leg skiing and is out for a few weeks. I don't really have anyone else who can do this kind of work. He won't be back for at least a week.

- *You:* How far did he get before he left for the ski trip?

- *Kumar:* He had worked out the major conclusions, but had just started the detailed report.

- *You:* That helps. If you can give me the work he did, I will use the "headlines" in my report. If my manager wants the detail, we'll have time to work it out. In a pinch, could you work on it? I'd be willing to cover you for your team meetings if you can put in enough time to give my boss something she can live with—only if she asks for it, of course.

- *Kumar:* That gives me some breathing room. I appreciate the offer, I was uncomfortable that I was letting you down.

- *You:* Thanks. I'd like the report, as it is, later today. I'll let you know if and when we need the supportive data.

2. Your teenage daughter, a bright and successful student, has announced that she will be turning down a scholarship to a prestigious university in favor of taking a year off to travel and

"find herself." You have had several heated arguments about this. Recently, you told her that you could not guarantee that you would pay her college tuition when she returned. Her response was that she was perfectly capable of earning her own money and attending a less expensive school. You feel that you have painted yourself into a corner and have not made any progress in convincing her of the importance to her future of making the right college choice. You are also concerned about her safety as a solo traveler in certain parts of the world.

You suspect that the approach you have been taking with your daughter has polarized both of you on the issue. You decide to take a fresh approach. You invite her out to lunch and begin a conversation with her. Your goal is to get her to agree to reconsider her plans.

- *You:* I believe I have been pretty unproductive in the way I have talked with you about your plans. I was thinking that, if I were in your shoes, I'd probably be more convinced than ever that I needed to make an independent decision about it.

- *Daughter:* I'm not trying to go against what you say. I just believe that I need to take time out from going to school right now. It's been a pretty intense year and I need a break.

- *You:* Help me understand what this trip would mean for you.

- *Daughter:* I just want some time to figure out what I want to do. I feel as if I've been meeting everyone else's expectations for a long time and I'm not sure any more that I want to do the things that other people want for me.

- *You:* So you want a little time and space to get to know yourself away from parents and teachers . . .

- *Daughter:* Exactly.

- *You:* What are some options for making that happen in addition to the solo trip you are thinking about?

- *Daughter:* I might be able to talk Sarah into going with me . . .

- *You:* What else might work?

- *Daughter:* I'm not sure . . .

- *You:* I know that the community college offers some small group tours for young people. Would that be an option?

- *Daughter:* It would depend. I'm not interested in "if it's Tuesday, it must be Paris" kind of tours.

- *You:* Another possibility might be to opt for the "Sophomore Year Abroad" program at the school that wants you . . .

- *Daughter:* I did like the sound of that.

- *You:* Would you consider trying the school for a year, preparing for that year abroad? If you would do that, I'd be willing to pay for a summer trip with a group this year, as long as you and I can agree on one that is reputable and affordable.

- *Daughter:* I will think it over. It sounds pretty good, but I need to make my own decision about it.

- *You:* I trust you to do that. It's hard for me to let go, but you really are an adult now. Let's talk about it later in the week.

3. You are a senior executive who is charged with the responsibility for implementing the final steps in merging two companies. Executives of the other firm, who see this as an acquisition by your company, rather than a merger, are dragging their feet in regard to aligning their systems with yours. They give you excuses that sound rational, but the net effect is to delay the implementation. You are under a lot of pressure to complete this. The new, merged systems should have been up and running by now, and you are feeling very frustrated and angry.

You have decided to meet with your counterpart from the other company to see whether you can enlist her help in merging the systems. You set a time and meet her at her office.

- *You:* Thanks for meeting with me, Heather. I'd like to talk about some issues regarding merging our HR and information systems.

- *Heather:* Well, I am really quite busy, so I can't take more than a few minutes today.

- *You:* Heather, I really need your help on this. I'm really puzzled about how to proceed. I don't seem to be getting very far. What do you think is holding the process up?

- *Heather:* Well, everyone is so busy, with the merger and all . . .

- *You:* Heather, I know how busy all of you are. Frankly, I'm concerned that we won't be ready by the time the merger is set to be final. I will personally have to go to the CEO next week and tell him that we are not on track, and I am not looking forward to that. I expect him to be pretty upset, and I would imagine that we will all feel the brunt of that. At least I know I will. So that is why I would like your help. I'm thinking that people may be concerned about learning the new systems. Could that be the issue?

- *Heather:* I don't really think that's it. Everyone on the leadership team is committed to making this work. The problem is, we got everyone in the company involved in designing and implementing our current system. It took a lot of time. They were really committed to it. And now they see this new one as being imposed on them. We are having a lot of resistance from some of our best people. They see it as a sign that this is an acquisition, not a merger. They are putting their resumes out on the street. It's all we can do to get through the day without a crisis. You know, people really put their hearts and souls into growing this company.

- *You:* So you are concerned about losing good people if they see that their commitment and loyalty may not be repaid.

- *Heather:* Yes. They are pretty demoralized.

- *You:* Do you have any ideas about what might help?

- *Heather:* I think it might help if they knew that nobody would be downsized. Your company has committed to that, but they don't trust the words.

- *You:* What if we put together a committee from both companies to start the process of merging the info system? You could include the informal leaders of the company and it would be a way for them to get to know their counterparts.

- *Heather:* That might be good, although they may not be very enthusiastic about volunteering.

- *You:* Are you thinking that they might worry about appearing to be "co-opted" by the big guys?

- *Heather:* You've got it.

- *You:* Here's my suggestion. Let's put together an "all-hands" meeting for both companies. We can lead it together and invite questions and concerns from the audience. I think that our attitude might well help resolve some of their concerns. We could then ask for volunteers to serve on the committee.

- *Heather:* That sounds like a reasonable way to go . . .

4. You have volunteered to help plan and host the yearly fundraiser for your child's preschool. You were reluctant to take this on for fear that you might end up, as has happened before, doing it all yourself. The first few meetings of your committee were very positive; several people volunteered to take responsibility for specific tasks. Now it is two weeks before the event, and several important things have not happened. Everyone has an excuse for not delivering on his

or her commitments. You feel that the staff and board are depending on you, and you don't want to let them down. This experience has convinced you, however, that you are not cut out for community leadership. You feel burned out and disappointed.

You are determined to get some help to bring this event off. You decide to call one of the committee members and see what you can do to get him or her to recommit.

- *You:* Hello, Chris. I'm glad I reached you. I need to talk with you about the fundraiser.

- *Chris:* I am so sorry that I haven't been able to come through on that. I have been completely swamped at work. I just didn't anticipate that, and I feel bad about it. In fact, I'm embarrassed.

- *You:* I know that you really want to help. You have been a real supporter of the school, and I believe that you are completely committed to making this a success.

- *Chris:* Yes, but I just can't do what I originally promised.

- *You:* Here's what's going on for me. The catering decisions and the follow-up calls to the presenters are really overdue. I am afraid that we will get to the day and find that we have no food and no speakers. There are several other things that I'm trying to do after work, but frankly, if I don't have help, some things won't be done, and we'll all be really disappointed. And I'm going to have a lot of egg on my face as the chair. . . . Chris, what would it take for you to take on one of those tasks?

- *Chris:* If you can give me the speakers' phone numbers or e-mail addresses, I'll take on the task of preparing them. I didn't realize that we were so far behind.

- *You:* Thanks, that will help a lot.

5. You have been nurturing an idea for a couple of years now. It would be an application of your current technology that you believe would have a tremendous impact on the market. It would require a moderate commitment of resources, but the payoff could be spectacular. The problem is that such a project is outside of your current area of responsibility and, in fact, might be seen as competitive with another group's current project. Your manager has already told you that you would have to have it approved and funded elsewhere; you suspect it is a political "hot potato." You are still hoping that someone will recognize the potential and support it, but you are discouraged.

You decide to go, with your manager's approval, to the senior manager who is accountable for both groups. Your goal is to influence her to agree to sponsor the idea and provide funding. You have asked your manager to set up the meeting and you are well prepared. You have just finished explaining the proposal to her.

- *You:* What questions do you have about my proposal?

- *Barbara:* How do you propose to fund the project? We don't have any budget for something like this.

- *You:* In my proposal, I talked about some ways to minimize costs by sharing facilities with another project. I believe that the project will more than pay for itself within two years. Given the need we've been hearing for diversifying our product line, this could look good to the board. What could I do that would convince you to take this on?

- *Barbara:* I do like the idea. I might be willing to bring it up at the next executive committee meeting to see whether we might find some special funding for it. That would be very difficult, though. Can you create a ten-minute presentation that summarizes benefits and costs? I would be willing to bring it up if I have something to show them.

- *You:* I'll get it to you by the end of the week. Let me know if I can help you prepare.

6. You were recently offered an exciting new position with your company. It would involve spending three years abroad and would probably lead to a significant role for you in the company's future. When you told your spouse about it, you expected enthusiastic support. Instead, you received a flat and resistant response. This surprised you, as you have always agreed that whichever one of you was offered the best opportunity would have the other's support, regardless of any inconvenience and disruption that might occur.

   You have just learned that your spouse is highly resistant to moving abroad, which will be required if you are to accept the new position. You expressed a lot of surprise and anger. Now you think that you had better pick yourself up, dust yourself off, and begin to explore the issues. Your goal is to influence your spouse to agree to consider the matter and give it a fair hearing, rather than refuse right away.

   - *You:* I really overreacted just then. I was truly surprised by your refusal, and I didn't respond very well. I need to listen to your concerns. What kind of problems would this create for you?

   - *Spouse:* Well, in the first place, I'm at a really critical place in my project right now, and it would be career-limiting to leave in the middle of it. And I don't like the idea of moving the kids out of their school. It's been very hard to find a school that works well for both of them.

   - *You:* So there are two main issues: what would happen to your career and how the kids would cope with another new school?

   - *Spouse:* Yes. I know we agreed to trade off on this, but that was before we were really settled and had a family. The situation is different now.

- *You:* And specifically, that is mainly because we have kids, as you see it . . .

- *Spouse:* And because we both are pretty committed to our current jobs.

- *You:* What do you see as the options we have now?

- *Spouse:* One possibility might be to see whether you could start by working from here and going over once a month or so. That would be the least disruptive.

- *You:* What else might work?

- *Spouse:* Well, I can see that I'll have more flexibility in about six months. I could think about a short-term move. But only if we could make it work for the kids.

- *You:* So your suggestion is that I see whether I can get them to agree to a start-up period where I'd be based here. If I do that, you'd be willing to consider a later move.

- *Spouse:* Yes. I really need to have some time to get used to the idea, of course. And to do some research on schools and possible jobs for me. I do want to keep our agreement, but I'm just not ready to make a complete commitment.

- *You:* I really appreciate you working this through with me. I'm pretty optimistic that we can work something out, if I can get my manager to be flexible.

7. You are the leader for an important project for your company. The project is not going as well as you had hoped. There is a lot of conflict, and milestones are not being achieved. You were selected for this role because of your technical skills, but what is dragging you down is just the day-to-day hassle of dealing with people's egos and working out the turf issues that seem to get in the way of every cross-functional team you have worked with.

You decide to meet with a key member of your team. Your goal is to influence him to agree to help you with the "people issues" on the team.

- *You:* Thanks for taking the time to meet with me. I'll get right to the point and tell you that I need some advice from you. You seem to me to have a lot of success in getting your group to work together. Your people skills have always impressed me. I'd like to see our whole team operating as well together as your part of the team does. I could really use your help in getting past the "turf issues" that are getting in our way.

- *Terry:* I do have a group that works well together. I'm not sure that has much to do with me . . .

- *You:* Terry, I see you as a real catalyst for that. You seem to know how to keep people aligned toward a common goal. I can imagine how effective we could be as a team if everyone were focused on the overall goal, and I can see you as key to making that happen.

- *Terry:* Well, I'm willing to work with you, but as a peer, I'm pretty limited in what I can say or do. I think it will require a change in process as well as a change in attitude.

- *You:* You sound concerned that people will think you are taking on too broad a role. Is that it?

- *Terry:* Yes, I don't want to limit my effectiveness by looking like I'm angling for a bigger role.

- *You:* What if you were to help me plan a team meeting? My meetings are usually pretty technical. I'm not experienced in looking at team process. They don't teach you how to do that in engineering school. Would you be willing to do that?

- *Terry:* Sure. I'll help you plan a meeting as long as you are clearly in charge of it.

- *You:* I'll be very clear that it is my meeting. In exchange, would you be willing to facilitate it?

- *Terry:* Sure, I can do that.

8. You are chairing a standards task force for your association that could make a major impact on the conduct of your profession. Some members of the group are very resistant to the idea of mandatory compliance with the standards. You and several others believe that it is an exercise in futility to develop and present standards and then let people choose whether to adopt them or not. The differences have divided the group, which has now reached an impasse. If you do not come to an agreement, the entire exercise will be seen as a waste of time, and you feel that you will lose the respect of your colleagues, both within the task force and outside of it; they have been counting on you to resolve this issue.

   You decide to begin the next meeting by confronting the issue in a way that you hope will be productive. Your goal is to influence a key colleague to reconsider his or her opposition.

   - *You:* I want to acknowledge the good news about what we have done so far. I think I have not been appreciative enough that we've been able to reach agreement on professional standards. That is really quite an accomplishment, and everyone has worked hard to make it happen. I'm hoping that by the end of the meeting today, we'll be a lot closer to agreement about how to implement those standards. I'd like to start by asking those of you who have been supporting the idea of voluntary compliance to say what your major concern is about making them mandatory.

   - *Colleague:* We've been through all that. Mainly, the issue is that our professional values are really opposed to coercion, and mandatory standards would seem very bureaucratic to the members. Also, I think that there are some very good people in the profession whose training would not come up to the standards we are recommending.

- *You:* So you're concerned that some key people would not meet the standards.

- *Colleague:* Yes, but the coercion issue is also important.

- *You:* What could we do that would make it possible for you to support a stricter implementation of the standard? How could we modify it so you could live with it?

- *Colleague:* Clearly, we'd have to have a "grandfather and grandmother" rule: anyone who has been in the society for more than a few years would not have to meet the standards.

- *You:* What else could we do that would make it possible for you to support enforcing the standards?

- *Colleague:* I'm not sure . . .

- *You:* What if we were to open up the process—to have the standards approved by most of the membership and to agree to a review after two years?

- *Colleague:* That would begin to meet some of my concerns. . . .

Notes

1. *Exercising Influence: Building Relationships and Getting Results* is a copyrighted program of Barnes & Conti Associates, Inc. For more information, see www.barnesconti.com/

2. Thomas Pickering, an expert on hypertension at Columbia University, says that the worst work-related stress is caused by jobs that offer people little power over their daily activities.

3. Aikido is a Japanese martial art, using principles similar to those of judo. It was developed in the 20th Century by Morihei Ueshiba. The word, in Japanese, means "the way of harmony with the universe."

4. The Myers Briggs Type Indicator is copyrighted and trademarked by Consulting Psychologists Press, Inc.

5. B. Kim Barnes. (2007). *Exercising Influence Workbook: A Self-Study Guide.* San Francisco: Pfeiffer.

6. Beckhard, R., & Harris, R.T. (1987). *Organizational Transitions: Managing Complex Change, 2nd Edition.* Boston: Addison-Wesley.

7. Malcolm Gladwell, in his book *The Tipping Point,* discusses this topic in an entertaining and informative way.

8. Ram Charan & Geoffrey Colvin. (1999, June 21). Why CEOs fail. *Fortune.*

Resources

Workshops and Seminars

Exercising Influence: Building Relationships and Getting Results. Barnes & Conti Associates, Inc., 800.835.0911, www.barnesconti.com.

Constructive Debate: Building Better Ideas. Barnes & Conti Associates, Inc., 800.835.0911, www.barnesconti.com.

Constructive Negotiation: Building Agreements That Work. Barnes & Conti Associates, Inc., 800.835.0911, www.barnesconti.com.

Inspirational Leadership: Encouraging Others to Do Great Things. Barnes & Conti Associates, Inc., 800.835.0911, www.barnesconti.com.

Facilitating Forward: Guiding Others Toward Results. Barnes & Conti Associates, Inc., 800.835.0911, www.barnesconti.com.

Graphic Facilitation (for meetings). The Grove Consultants, Inc., 800.494.7683, www.grove.com.

Facilitative Leadership (for meetings). Interaction Associates, Inc., 415.241.8000, www.interactionassociates.com.

Instrument

Myers-Briggs Type Indicator. Consulting Psychologists Press, Inc., 415.326.0255, www.mbti.com.

Additional Reading

Cialdini, Robert B. (1993). *Influence: The psychology of persuasion.* New York: William Morrow.

Emerson, Ralph Waldo. (1991). *Self-reliance.* New York: Bell Tower.

Fisher, Roger, & Sharp, Alan. (1998). *Getting it done: How to lead when you are not in charge.* New York: HarperCollins.

Gladwell, Malcolm. (2000). *The tipping point: How little things can make a big difference.* Boston: Little Brown.

Goleman, Daniel. (1998). *Working with emotional intelligence.* New York: Bantam Books.

Hogan, Kevin. (2004). *The psychology of persuasion: How to persuade others to your way of thinking.* Gretna, LA: Pelican Publishing.

Kouzes, James M., & Posner, Barry Z. (2005). *The leadership challenge* (3rd ed.). San Francisco: Jossey-Bass.

Maurer, Rick. (2002). *Why don't you want what I want? How to win support for your ideas without hard sell, manipulation, or power plays.* Houston, TX: Bard Press.

Tannen, Deborah. (1998). *The argument culture: Stopping America's war of words.* New York: Ballantine.

Special Issues in Influence

Index

Index

About the Author

B. KIM BARNES is co-founder and CEO of Barnes & Conti Associates, Inc., a learning and organization development firm in Berkeley, California. Her company specializes in moving ideas into action through influence and innovation. Kim has been interested in how people communicate and influence throughout her long professional life as a teacher, trainer, organizational consultant, executive coach, course developer, writer, leader, and entrepreneur, as well as in her personal life as a spouse, partner, mother, grandmother, and friend.

Kim is a frequent speaker at national and international professional conferences and meetings and has published many articles in the United States and abroad. She is the primary developer of *Exercising Influence, Constructive Negotiation, Constructive Debate, Inspirational Leadership, Intelligent Risk-Taking, Managing Innovation* (with David Francis), *Creating a Culture for Risk and Innovation, The Mastery of Change, The Art of Communication, Leading Global and Virtual Teams,* and other copyrighted programs of Barnes & Conti Associates, Inc.

For more information on these or any other Barnes & Conti programs and services, visit www.barnesconti.com.

Barnes & Conti Associates, Inc.

Was established in 1985 to meet the challenging and Changing needs of individuals and organizations through our public and in-house seminars and programs. To succeed, you must be able to share information and move ideas into action more rapidly than ever before.

Barnes & Conti partners with our customers as a virtual team member to achieve ongoing learning and innovation.

Barnes & Conti provides flexible, just-in-time programs and services that add real value and help customers achieve extraordinary business results.

All Barnes & Conti programs can be presented in a varietyof formats for intact teams or as open sessions:

- Customizable, hands-on, intensive workshops
- Distance learning, including web meetings
- "Learning interventions," focusing on real and current work
- Site licensing for classroom or intranet delivery

Some of our courses include:

- Exercising Influence

- Constructive Debate

- Managing Innovation

- Strategic Thinking

- Inspirational Leadership

- Art of Communication

- Leading Global and Virtual Teams

- Intelligent Risk Taking

- Creating a Culture for Risk and Innovation

- Mastery of Change

- Facilitating Forward

At Barnes & Conti our promises to our clients and partners are:

1. To understand your organization's mission, vision, people, processes, and issues.

2. To provide the highest quality programs and services designed to meet the learning needs that support high performance and excellent business results for your organization.

3. To be flexible, friendly, and fast in responding to you.

4. To support you in applying the skills to real business issues in your world.

5. To be clear, fair, ethical, and business-like with you about scope, deliverables, pricing, and other condition of our agreements.

Please visit our website at www.barnesconti.com, or call 1-800-835-0911

Pfeiffer Publications Guide

This guide is designed to familiarize you with the various types of Pfeiffer publications. The formats section describes the various types of products that we publish; the methodologies section describes the many different ways that content might be provided within a product. We also provide a list of the topic areas in which we publish.

FORMATS

In addition to its extensive book-publishing program, Pfeiffer offers content in an array of formats, from fieldbooks for the practitioner to complete, ready-to-use training packages that support group learning.

FIELDBOOK Designed to provide information and guidance to practitioners in the midst of action. Most fieldbooks are companions to another, sometimes earlier, work, from which its ideas are derived; the fieldbook makes practical what was theoretical in the original text. Fieldbooks can certainly be read from cover to cover. More likely, though, you'll find yourself bouncing around following a particular theme, or dipping in as the mood, and the situation, dictate.

HANDBOOK A contributed volume of work on a single topic, comprising an eclectic mix of ideas, case studies, and best practices sourced by practitioners and experts in the field.

An editor or team of editors usually is appointed to seek out contributors and to evaluate content for relevance to the topic. Think of a handbook not as a ready-to-eat meal, but as a cookbook of ingredients that enables you to create the most fitting experience for the occasion.

RESOURCE Materials designed to support group learning. They come in many forms: a complete, ready-to-use exercise (such as a game); a comprehensive resource on one topic (such as conflict management) containing a variety of methods and approaches; or a collection of like-minded activities (such as icebreakers) on multiple subjects and situations.

TRAINING PACKAGE An entire, ready-to-use learning program that focuses on a particular topic or skill. All packages comprise a guide for the facilitator/trainer and a workbook for the participants. Some packages are supported with additional media—such as video—or learning aids, instruments, or other devices to help participants understand concepts or practice and develop skills.

- *Facilitator/trainer's guide* Contains an introduction to the program, advice on how to organize and facilitate the learning event, and step-by-step instructor notes. The guide also contains copies of presentation materials—handouts, presentations, and overhead designs, for example—used in the program.

- *Participant's workbook* Contains exercises and reading materials that support the learning goal and serves as a valuable reference and support guide for participants in the weeks and months that follow the learning event. Typically, each participant will require his or her own workbook.

ELECTRONIC CD-ROMs and web-based products transform static Pfeiffer content into dynamic, interactive experiences. Designed to take advantage of the searchability, automation, and ease-of-use that technology provides, our e-products bring convenience and immediate accessibility to your workspace.

METHODOLOGIES

CASE STUDY A presentation, in narrative form, of an actual event that has occurred inside an organization. Case studies are not prescriptive, nor are they used to prove a point; they are designed to develop critical analysis and decision-making skills. A case study has a specific time frame, specifies a sequence of events, is narrative in structure, and contains a plot structure—an issue (what should be/have been done?). Use case studies when the goal is to enable participants to apply previously learned theories to the circumstances in the case, decide what is pertinent, identify the real issues, decide what should have been done, and develop a plan of action.

ENERGIZER A short activity that develops readiness for the next session or learning event. Energizers are most commonly used after a break or lunch to stimulate or refocus the group. Many involve some form of physical activity, so they are a useful way to counter post-lunch lethargy. Other uses include transitioning from one topic to another, where "mental" distancing is important.

EXPERIENTIAL LEARNING ACTIVITY (ELA) A facilitator-led intervention that moves participants through the learning cycle from experience to application (also known as a Structured Experience). ELAs are carefully thought-out designs in which there is a definite learning purpose and intended outcome. Each step—everything that participants do during the activity—facilitates the accomplishment of the stated goal. Each ELA includes complete instructions for facilitating the intervention and a clear statement of goals, suggested group size and timing, materials required, an explanation of the process, and, where appropriate, possible variations to the activity. (For more detail on Experiential Learning Activities, see the Introduction to the *Reference Guide to Handbooks and Annuals*, 1999 edition, Pfeiffer, San Francisco.)

GAME A group activity that has the purpose of fostering team spirit and togetherness in addition to the achievement of a pre-stated goal. Usually contrived—undertaking a desert expedition, for example—this type of learning method offers an engaging means for participants to demonstrate and practice business and interpersonal skills. Games are effective for team building and personal development mainly because the goal is subordinate to the process—the means through which participants reach decisions, collaborate, communicate, and generate trust and understanding. Games often engage teams in "friendly" competition.

ICEBREAKER A (usually) short activity designed to help participants overcome initial anxiety in a training session and/or to acquaint the participants with one another. An icebreaker can be a fun activity or can be tied to specific topics or training goals. While a useful tool in itself, the icebreaker comes into its own in situations where tension or resistance exists within a group.

INSTRUMENT A device used to assess, appraise, evaluate, describe, classify, and summarize various aspects of human behavior. The term used to describe an instrument depends primarily on its format and purpose. These terms include survey, questionnaire, inventory, diagnostic, survey, and poll. Some uses of instruments include providing instrumental feedback to group members, studying here-and-now processes or functioning within a group, manipulating group composition, and evaluating outcomes of training and other interventions.

Instruments are popular in the training and HR field because, in general, more growth can occur if an individual is provided with a method for focusing specifically on his or her own behavior. Instruments also are used to obtain information that will serve as a basis for change and to assist in workforce planning efforts.

Paper-and-pencil tests still dominate the instrument landscape with a typical package comprising a facilitator's guide, which offers advice on administering the instrument and interpreting the collected data, and an initial set of instruments. Additional instruments are available separately. Pfeiffer, though, is investing heavily in e-instruments. Electronic instrumentation provides effortless distribution and, for larger groups particularly, offers advantages over paper-and-pencil tests in the time it takes to analyze data and provide feedback.

LECTURETTE A short talk that provides an explanation of a principle, model, or process that is pertinent to the participants' current learning needs. A lecturette is intended to establish a common language bond between the trainer and the participants by providing a mutual frame of reference. Use a lecturette as an introduction to a group activity or event, as an interjection during an event, or as a handout.

MODEL A graphic depiction of a system or process and the relationship among its elements. Models provide a frame of reference and something more tangible, and more easily remembered, than a verbal explanation. They also give participants something to "go on," enabling them to track their own progress as they experience the dynamics, processes, and relationships being depicted in the model.

ROLE PLAY A technique in which people assume a role in a situation/scenario: a customer service rep in an angry-customer exchange, for example. The way in which the role is approached is then discussed and feedback is offered. The role play is often repeated using a different approach and/or incorporating changes made based on feedback received. In other words, role playing is a spontaneous interaction involving realistic behavior under artificial (and safe) conditions.

SIMULATION A methodology for understanding the interrelationships among components of a system or process. Simulations differ from games in that they test or use a model that depicts or mirrors some aspect of reality in form, if not necessarily in content. Learning occurs by studying the effects of change on one or more factors of the model. Simulations are commonly used to test hypotheses about what happens in a system—often referred to as "what if?" analysis—or to examine best-case/worst-case scenarios.

THEORY A presentation of an idea from a conjectural perspective. Theories are useful because they encourage us to examine behavior and phenomena through a different lens.

TOPICS

The twin goals of providing effective and practical solutions for workforce training and organization development and meeting the educational needs of training and human resource professionals shape Pfeiffer's publishing program. Core topics include the following:

Leadership & Management

Communication & Presentation

Coaching & Mentoring

Training & Development

e-Learning

Teams & Collaboration

OD & Strategic Planning

Human Resources

Consulting

What will you find on pfeiffer.com?

- The best in workplace performance solutions for training and HR professionals

- Downloadable training tools, exercises, and content

- Web-exclusive offers

- Training tips, articles, and news

- Seamless on-line ordering

- Author guidelines, information on becoming a Pfeiffer Affiliate, and much more

Discover more at www.pfeiffer.com